Private Presses & Publishing in England since 1945

Gettysburg

Fourscore and seven years ago our fathers brought forth upon this continent a new nation, conceived in liberty, and dedicated to the proposition that all men are created equal. Now we are engaged in a great civil war, testing whether that nation, or any nation so conceived and so dedicated, can long endure. We are met on a great battle-field of that war. We have come to dedicate a portion of that field as a final resting-place for those who here gave their lives that that nation might live. It is altogether fitting and proper that we should do this. But in a larger sense we cannot dedicate, we cannot consecrate, we cannot hallow this ground. The brave men, living and dead, who struggled here, have consecrated it far above our power to add or detract. The world will little note nor long remember what we say here, but it can never forget what they did here. It is for us, the living, rather, to be dedicated here to the unfinished work which they who fought here have thus far so nobly advanced. It is rather for us to be here dedicated to the great task remaining before us; that from these honoured dead we take increased devotion to that cause for which they gave the last full measure of devotion; that we here highly resolve that these dead shall not have died in vain; that this nation, under God, shall have a new birth of freedom; & that government of the people, by the people, and for the people, shall not perish from the earth.   Abraham Lincoln

SET IN MONOTYPE GOUDY TEXT WITH TITLE LETTERING BY WILL CARTER

Frontispiece. *Gettysburg.* A broadsheet from Rampant Lions Press. Reproduced with the permission of Will Carter.

B. E. BELLAMY

*

*Private Presses &
Publishing in England
since 1945*

K · G · Saur   Clive Bingley
New York · London · München · Paris

First published 1980
by Clive Bingley Ltd, a member of
the K G Saur International Publishing Group.
Copyright © Bruce E Bellamy.
All rights reserved.
Set in 12 on 14 point Aldine Roman by Allset.
Printed and bound in the UK by
Redwood Burn Ltd of Trowbridge and Esher.
Bingley (UK) ISBN: 0-85157-297-9
Saur (USA) ISBN: 0-89664-180-5

British Library Cataloguing in Publication Data

Bellamy, B E
    Private presses & publishing in England since 1945.
    1. Private presses — England — History — 20th
    century
    I. Title
    338.4'7'68620942   Z231.5.P7

ISBN 0-85157-297-9

Contents

Illustrations	4
Foreword	5
Preface	7
Introduction	9

Part one THE HISTORICAL PERSPECTIVE

1 Origins	15
2 Survival and revival	31
3 A new movement	49
4 Poetry and the private press	67
5 A living tradition	79

Part two EIGHT CONTEMPORARY PRESSES

Preliminary note	95
6 The Cuckoo Hill Press	97
7 The Shoestring Press	100
8 The Keepsake Press	105
9 The Kit-Cat Press	108
10 Poet & Printer	113
11 The Plough Press	116
12 The Mandeville Press	119
13 The Basilisk Press and Bookshop	124

Part Three A MARKET AND ITS PROSPECTS

14 Reaching the customer	127
Bibliography	133
Appendix	144
Index	164

Illustrations

Frontispiece. *Gettysburg.* A broadsheet from Rampant Lions Press. Reproduced with the permission of Will Carter.

The Kelmscott Chaucer from the Basilisk Press. Reproduced with the permission of Charlene Garry.   25

Opening from *On printing by hand.* Reproduced with the permission of David Chambers.   40 / 41

Title page from *Anaglyptography.* Reproduced with the permission of Geoffrey Wakeman.   58

Opening from *Cornish Aerie.* Reproduced with the permission of Toni Savage, Richard Gilbertson and Rigby Graham.   76 / 77

Opening from *New Beginnings.* Reproduced with the permission of Alan Tarling and Eric Walter White.   84 / 85

Title page opening from *Dick and Sal at Canterbury Fair.* Reproduced with the permission of Ben Sands.   102 / 103

Opening from *Damon the mower.* Reproduced with the permission of Kenneth Hardacre.   110 / 111

Title page from *John Paas & James Cook.* Reproduced with the permission of Geoffrey Wakeman.   118

Opening from *Water Lane.* Reproduced with the permission of Peter Scupham.   122 / 123

Title page from *The Other Planet.* Reproduced with the permission of Roy Lewis.   132

Foreword
by Roderick Cave

In the years immediately after World War 2, the future of the private press—or whether it *had* a future at all—was debatable. The few survivors of the presses in the great Arts and Crafts tradition, such as the Golden Cockerel, were but shadows of their former selves. The prospects for other such ventures, with special proprietary typefaces and so on, were bleak in those austere years. It could have been argued (and was) that commercial book printers and typographers had learned all the lessons that could be learned from the private press movement: the word 'relevance' was not then bandied around in the hideous way that it has been since, but the relevance of presses using antiquated methods to produce expensive limited editions for a wealthy clientele was certainly questioned.

The future which seemed so promising to the optimists of the late forties has not developed in the ways anticipated. With the switch to photocomposition, offset-lithography and other changes in the book-printing field, and with the altered structure of commercial publishing over the past thirty years, it no longer seems as clear by any means that the lessons of the private press movement have been learned as thoroughly as was then thought. To what extent, and in what ways the average trade book of today is better or worse produced than that of 1950 is arguable, but it is certainly a very different thing.

The work of the private presses is also very different. The private press did not die, its mission completed, and it was an absurd misconception of the motives of private printers to expect them to disappear. Quite the contrary. By 1959 there were enough enthusiastic amateurs of printing (inspired by the writings of Stanley Morison, Beatrice Warde *et al.*, and in particular by John Ryder's *Printing for Pleasure*) for the Private Libraries Association to commence publication of its annual bibliography *Private Press Books*, and in the twenty years since then the movement has gained considerable strength. To a considerable extent, the contemporary private presses are closer in scale to the Victorian parlour printers, though in spirit and ideals they hark back to the Arts and Crafts Movement and the writers on typography mentioned above. Now that the printing trade has become technology rather than craft, it is heartening that there are those who keep the older skills and values alive. The private press today stands in something of the same position as the craft pottery to the ceramics industry: using old skills and old methods to manufacture articles which may be useful, may be beautiful, and which provide the manufacturers as well as the purchasers with a pleasure less easily achieved through larger scale industry. The presses do not represent every facet of alternative printing and publishing for the 'alternative society' by any means, but their work forms a significant part of worthwhile publishing outside the normal trade channels.

Librarianship's attitudes to private press work in the past has been ambivalent. The ideals of the public library and the conditions in which library services have developed did not make the expensive edition-de-luxe particularly attractive to acquisitions librarians. Today's more modest presses have often been overlooked for other reasons, some of them cogent: private press work today is typically 'difficult'—difficult to trace, often harder to buy, and when bought often in awkward formats and inadequate bindings.

Some libraries have made valiant attempts to acquire such material for their local or other special collections, but in general it is probably fair to say that private press work is a problem most of us have not faced squarely. For this reason alone it is particularly satisfying to me that the present study by a practising librarian should have originated as academic work in a school of librarianship, and should be published under this imprint. Although the literature on private presses is extensive, most of it is available only in specialist journals such as *The Private Library* or the American *Fine Print*, and it often has an inbred quality, being written for enthusiasts by enthusiasts. An independent survey by someone outside the field is very welcome.

Bruce Bellamy's sampler of contemporary private press activity is limited to the British Isles. The presses he has chosen to illustrate such activity are however representative of a far larger group. Some of the work being produced in Australia, Canada, New Zealand or the United States can be sampled through the stock of a few specialist dealers; that produced by private printers in the Netherlands, Italy and other countries is harder to find, but it is surprisingly similar in type. And there is enough of it to give the lie to those who predict the death of the book and anticipate the paperless society with relish. Amateur typefounding is undertaken in the United States; some amateurs build their own presses, and increasing numbers are moving towards making their own paper. The private press will continue to flourish and to produce publications with a good reason for existing—and for being held in libraries.

Preface

It is impossible in a book of this length to attempt a comprehensive account of private printing since 1945. In this period more than 600 presses have been active in England. Nonetheless important developments can be traced and significant trends identified. The objectives have been threefold: to examine the varied nature of private publishing and printing presses in England; to describe the way in which they have developed during the last thirty years; and to discover what their relationships are with the commercial printing and publishing industries.

A description of the means by which the area of study was delineated is followed by a brief account of the problems associated with the literature of the subject, and the methods by which this project was brought to completion. The history of private presses in England is given in outline, from the mid-eighteenth century until the outbreak of the second world war. This is followed by a series of brief accounts of private printers who started printing before 1945, survived the war and continued printing afterwards. The revival of fine printing in the late 1940s and early 1950s is then brought up to the beginnings of the new private press movement. Developments in private printing in the late 1950s are dealt with in some detail and progress is followed into the early 1960s. Poetry publishing by private presses is discussed and examined in some detail. The chronicle of events is continued into the 1970s.

Throughout those chapters covering the period since the beginning of the new movement, the development of public interest in the products of the private presses is kept in view, and particular emphasis is placed on exhibitions of private press books. A selection of contemporary presses is then described in detail to reveal the variety of motives and differences in approach adopted by the respective printers. Finally the problems of finding the markets for private press books are analysed and a number of solutions to these problems are discussed. The general conclusions of the study indicate that private presses are thriving and attracting more interest now than at any time since the mid-1950s.

Dependence upon the work of so many other writers in the field cannot be over emphasised, and I would like to thank the following people particularly, for all the help and encouragement they have given me: Roderick Cave for answering all my questions and listening sympathetically as my knowledge of the subject developed; David Chambers, Charlene Garry, Rigby Graham, Kenneth Hardacre, Roy Lewis, Ben Sands, Toni Savage, Peter Scupham, Alan Tarling, and Geoffrey Wakeman for generously giving me their time, and dealing so patiently with my enquiries about their printing activities; the library staff at the Library Association and St Bride Printing Library for obtaining books, periodical articles and photocopies from their stocks; David Jones and his staff in the Request Services Section of Hillingdon Borough Libraries for locating and obtaining the more difficult items; and finally my wife for typing the completed text.

Introduction

The subject matter of this book has been made more manageable by using John Ryder's classification of private presses to establish its boundaries. This classification was first outlined in 'The Contemporary Private Press' which was published as Appendix C in Glaister's *Glossary of the book* (1960). Ryder divided private presses into five groups:

I   *Publishing*
II Teaching
III Experimental
IV *Printing*
V   Clandestine

These classes are far from being clear cut, for many of the presses considered below fall into two or more of them. Nonetheless by bringing together publishing and printing presses a well-populated and most interesting field of study is revealed. Using this scheme also helps to clarify the terminology in both this and the surrounding territory. Such categorisations as small presses, little presses, independent publishers and private presses are used almost interchangeably, creating confusion that is otherwise impossible to clear up adequately. By linking classes I and IV it becomes possible to include most of the private presses which have flourished in England during the last three decades. Private publishing and printing presses in religious orders have been excluded from consideration because of work done at Sheffield University by Suzanne Oakes in her study *Monastic printing presses past and present* (1974).

The present work is based on Roderick Cave's *The Private*

Press Faber & Faber 1971, particularly chapter 18, 'World War Two and the Aftermath', and chapter 19, 'The Contemporary Scene in Britain'. It is hoped that the treatment developed here will complement and expand some of the themes only briefly touched on in that book and further will include developments which have take place in the 1970s. The presses of the post-war period are in direct line of descent from the central tradition of private press history. The three principal strands from William Blake, Henry Daniel and William Morris are reviewed and shown to be of continuing relevance.

The sphere of the private press contrasts sharply with that of the modern publishing and printing industry. The latter is geared to mass production, logically, because the book printed from moveable types was only the earliest example of an apparently unending series of modern technological artefacts. The enormous outpouring of books and documents is essential to the smooth functioning of modern society, but in many ways it is unresponsive to the needs of the individual. Caught in the backwash of advancing technology some people tend to look for older, more responsive and in some respects simpler techniques through which to achieve satisfaction.

The hand-printing press is one device which meets the requirements of these people, some of whom only want to pursue an absorbing hobby and print for their own pleasure. It is equally appropriate for artists reproducing their own linocuts, wood engravings or line blocks, while other artists find fulfilment by making complete books: selecting the paper, writing the text, selecting an appropriate typeface or calligraphic hand which will blend harmoniously with their illustrations and finally binding the sheets in the manner which is most suitable for the achievement of the end they have in view.

Another avenue is followed by some private printers who print contemporary poetry—which is occasionally very good —for poets who would otherwise not be published because the commercial market regards such work as unprofitable. These small books of poetry also provide an outlet for artists to produce illustrations which blend with the text, and the publisher-printer derives satisfaction not only from making these books but also from contributing to the continued survival of literary and artistic culture.

In essence the modern private press is altruistic, and of all the many definitions and descriptions of the private press the best is the idealistic affirmation made by Will Ransom in the opening chapter of *Private Presses and their Books* (1929);

> 'a private press may be defined as the typographic expression of a personal ideal, conceived in freedom and maintained in independence'.

However there are pitfalls to be avoided. Printing with one's own press can lead to the worst forms of egotism and self indulgence, and the whole thing can become trapped in narcissism. Another problem is presented by one of the more widespread modern obsessions, the cult of craft. It is almost as if the very decay of displaced crafts generates sentiment for them. Nostalgia for passing things leads to their attempted revival, and what was once difficult and sometimes dangerous work becomes desirable and apparently enjoyable to those who would never have considered such drudgery when it was part of day-to-day living. Fortunately private printing seems by and large to have escaped this sort of 'archeology' and to have come into the hands of dedicated and idiosyncratic craftsmen. They are not all amateur printers. Some of them are full-time printers, printing executives or typographers who also enjoy printing at home in their spare time.

The sources of information in printed form on private presses tend, for the most part, to be concentrated in a small number of bibliographies, books and journals. The remaining relatively small portion of material is spread intermittently through a very wide range of journals, magazines, daily and weekly newspapers. By no means everything that is available is recorded and indexed, and a proportion of items included in the bibiography have been discovered by chance. Much of the material consists of short descriptive articles where no attempt is made to probe in depth the reasons for the continued existence of private presses in the late twentieth century. Occasional pieces do examine such matters at length and these have been drawn on and supplemented in the following work. The principal method of enriching the documentary sources has been to conduct lengthy interviews with the printers from presses included in Part Two—'Eight contemporary private presses'. Every available opportunity has been taken to examine and collect books and pamphlets printed by the private presses discussed below. The Basilisk Press and Bookshop, which holds stock from several dozen private presses, offers a unique opportunity for comparison of items from the different printers, as well as providing collectors with the opportunity of examining interesting items before purchase. The St Bride Printing Library has a useful collection of private press books that can be seen on request.

Part one

THE HISTORICAL PERSPECTIVE

Chapter one

ORIGINS

The earliest example of English private printing might be said to date from 1474 when William Caxton was a member of the household of the Duchess of Burgundy, sister of King Edward IV in Bruges. Some years earlier, when Caxton held the appointment of 'Goverer of the English Nation' in Utrecht and Bruges, he had begun work on a translation of Raoul le Fevre's *Recueil des histoires de Troyes* which he had set aside incomplete. He showed the Duchess his work and was commanded to finish it. The demand for copies of his translation was such that he resorted to learning how to print in order to satisfy his friends and patrons.

However the real beginnings of the private press in England lie in the middle of the eighteenth century when an aristocrat, Horace Walpole, who was one of the most civilized men of the time, founded the Strawberry Hill Press at his villa in Twickenham. It was inaugurated in the summer of 1757 and the first printer, William Robinson, remained with Walpole for two years. The 'first fruits' of the press were two of Thomas Gray's *Odes* that Walpole said he had snatched from the hands of Robert Dodsley, the bookseller, who was on the point of preparing them for publication. Gray and Walpole had been friends almost continuously since being at Eton together. After Robinson left, the press suffered frequent changes of printer until 1765. In that year Walpole appointed Thomas Kirgate and there began an association which was to last until Walpole's death in 1797. The press continued in operation until 1789 and in that time a considerable number of Walpole's own works were printed, including *The Mysterious Mother* (1768) and *Hieroglyphic Tales* (1785). It also provided Walpole with entertainment, and attractive trifles were often printed for the amusement of house guests. Like many modern private press owners, Walpole derived much pleasure from his printing office.

Almost contemporaneous but of a very different character were the printing activities of the poet William Blake. Apprenticed by enlightened parents to a master engraver, James Basire, at the age of fifteen, he spent the next seven years working loyally for his master and in the process becoming a fully trained copper plate engraver. On completion of his apprenticeship he possessed a sound basic skill which enabled him to find work and a meagre living through the long years while his poetic and artistic talents were maturing. His aim was to blend an etched calligraphic text with tempera paintings on the same page in such a way that each 'illuminated' the other. He was able to complete very few copies of each of his works, and then only to order, for after printing he coloured each copy by hand. His work exhibits a continuous development, from the simple, graphic pages of *Songs of Innocence* (1789), through *Songs of Experience* (1790-1794), *Visions of the Daughters of Albion* (1793), *Milton, A Poem* (1804-1808), and ultimately, to the most complete expression of his genius as poet, printer and prophet, the magnificently executed *Jerusalem: the emanation of the giant Albion* (1804-1818).

His methods of book production had only been arrived at through years of very great and sustained effort. His visionary works were never popular because he was very much ahead of his time, and he was only sustained by his devoted wife Catherine and a few steady friends and patrons. Most of the time he managed to support himself and his wife by producing illustrations for books and prints which he was able to sell to a few interested customers. His influence was slow in growing and it has only become widespread during the twentieth century. He is the source of inspiration for the first important and still flourishing strand in the private press tradition—that of the artist possessed of both literary and graphic talents who finds fulfilment in making his own books, often eschewing the use of printing type for the text, and developing very complicated reproduction processes to achieve a desired effect.

In the nineteenth century a new element appeared in the history of private printing. The prosperous middle classes, with a progressively increasing amount of leisure time on their hands, were induced by astute commercial interests to take up home printing for their amusement and further enlightenment. This development had been made possible by a major improvement in printing press technology. Until the end of the eighteenth century there had been no essential changes in the wooden hand-press. Even Baskerville's improvements only increased its precision when taking an impression. The turning-point came with a change in the material used for constructing the hand-press. The third Earl of Stanhope perfected the first iron printing press in 1800, which combined the screw principle of the common wooden press with a lever action, thus increasing the pressure exerted by the platen and quickening its operation. From Stanhope's invention there came a wide range of improved iron presses, the best of which was the Albion press devised by R W Cope of London in 1823. This is the most perfect flat bed hand-press ever built and many, manufactured in the nineteenth century, are still in use today.

For the parlour printer, however, it was not the full size Albions which were important, but the range of table top models which were produced to meet the growing demand for scaled down printing equipment suitable for use in the home. Prior to these and other successful developments in miniaturizing the hand-press, as Cave writes in *The Private*

Press:

> For the average man looking for a recreation, the lack of a satisfactory, simple and portable press was enough to prevent him from taking up printing at all.

In the 1830s Messrs Holtzapffel & Co, an engineering equipment manufacturer, were advertising printing presses 'on the Stanhope and other principles in small sizes', and they were able to build up a thriving business selling printing equipment to home printers. One of their most popular presses for the family was the mahogany Parlour press invented by Edward Cowper, which had a horizontal bed and hinged platen that was pressed downwards by a lever employing a knuckle joint to produce a satisfactory impression. Another hand operated miniature press made in Great Britain by the Model Printing Press Company, some examples of which are still in operation today, was derived from the commercial treadle platen machine, and it became very popular with the home printer. In these machines the chase was held vertically with the platen hinged to its lower edge. It printed with a clam-like action, in a manner not dissimilar to that of the horizontal parlour press. The popularity of home printing continued to grow throughout the middle decades of the century, reaching its zenith between 1875 and 1885. It was about this time that photography became more accessible to the amateur, and possibly as a result of this the interest in printing declined among the middle classes. The modern successor to Messrs Holtzapffel and the Model Printing Press Company is Adana (Printing Machines) Ltd of Twickenham, and they continue to supply the printing equipment needs of some of the modern private presses.

Today there are nothing like so many people printing in their own homes as there were in Victorian times, but the generally high standard of printing which is being maintained by contemporary presses is a result of the influence of two men of very different characters. The first, and probably most significant for the late twentieth century private press movement, is C H O Daniel who printed his books at home with his family. In doing so he raised the standards of parlour printing to a level where the books he made will bear comparison with the best modern commercial printers. The second is William Morris—a socialist, novelist, poet, teacher, interior designer, prime mover in the 'Arts and Crafts Movement', and many other things besides. In the last years of his life, turning his attention to printing, he became one of the greatest and most influential of the private printers because of the books he caused to be printed while proprietor of the Kelmscott press.

The Reverend C H O Daniel was born in 1836 at Frome in Somerset where his father was vicar. He began printing as a boy in a primitive fashion, inking the types with his thumb and impressing them by hand. His father, approving these activities, presented Charles and his brother with what was probably a Holtzapffel Parlour press, and they continued printing until Charles went to boarding school. He did not return to printing for three years, but when in the summer of 1850 he was given a miniature Albion press he began printing his father's sermons, some small pamphlets and also a small amount of jobbing printing for the parish. He returned to school in 1853 and in 1854 went to Worcester College, Oxford. After teaching for a few years he accepted a fellowship from his old college, and returned to Oxford in 1863, living there for the rest of his life. It was not from any wish to improve anyone or anything that Daniel worked at his press: it was because he derived a great deal of enjoyment from the making of books.

When he returned home after a visit to Frome in 1874,

bearing the Albion press and type, his interest rekindled, he began printing once again. His enthusiasm eventually led to the involvement of his wife and daughters in the making of books. Together they seem to represent the finest exemplar of the Victorian family devoted to parlour printing. There was however much more to the Daniel Press than this.

Daniel, like William Blake, is the originator of one of the living strands in the private press tradition. This is because, quite accidentally, he rediscovered the Fell types in Oxford and then printed some excellent books with them at home. These types, purchased by Dean Fell from Holland in the seventeenth century, had been used to improve the quality of books printed at the University Press. Later on they had unfortunately fallen into disuse and been forgotten. In the early part of 1876, after he had examined the Fell types and come to admire them, Daniel bought some from the University. Once he had acquired them he continued using these types for his own printing throughout his life. His first major success with them was *The garland for Rachel* (1881) celebrating his daughter's first birthday. It included, among other contributions, poems from Edmund Gosse, Lewis Carroll and Robert Bridges, making up an impressive garland of contemporary literary talent. It was also a sound piece of book production, beautifully printed and well bound, with the pages illuminated by Mrs Daniel. Thirty-six copies were printed and the seventeen contributors were each presented with one. It was very well received and Daniel, encouraged by his achievement, purchased a large Albion press in the winter of 1881-1882. He experimented briefly with short pieces which satisfied him and in 1883 published *Sixe Idillia* by Theocritus, offering copies for sale to the public. For the next twenty years he continued to produce excellent books including a number of first editions of the work of Robert Bridges. Altogether he printed fifty-two books in his spare time while working as Bursar for his college. His wife and daughters assisted him and on occasion produced complete books themselves. He closed the press in 1903 when elected Provost of Worcester College. After Daniel's death a bibliography of books from the Press was printed at the Bodleian Library, where his Albion press is still to be seen in a special printing room.

Books from the Daniel Press are refreshingly simple, reflecting the influence of the revitalized seventeenth century typography which had been engendered by the energetic Dr Fell. Many of the better modern private presses strive for a similar effect, without necessarily looking backwards, but they derive their impulse from closely related aesthetic principles, and in so doing are continuing along the path first taken by the Reverend Daniel.

During the time that Daniel was working quite independently in Oxford and producing his best work, in London a movement was gathering strength for an assault on what it regarded as the decadent state of book printing then existing in England. As with many other revolutions, the leaders of this one concentrated their attentions upon what was clearly very wrong with, in this case, book production, while choosing to ignore what was good, castigating the whole of English printing without exception. That much of what was being printed at the end of the nineteenth century was feeble and uninspiring is not in doubt. A reaffirmation of what had been good was needed, but there were a number of commercial presses, including the Chiswick Press, R & R Clark, and T & A Constable, producing sound books. These were the exceptions however and generally book production was in an unhealthy condition. The movement for radical change in English printing had its origins in the much wider 'Arts and Crafts Movement' which sought to bring the dignity of art to craft and the vigour of craft to art. Of its many manifestations, that which took up the cause of the 'book beautiful' has probably had the most widespread effect. The leader of this crusade was a man of many talents who turned to printing after a life filled with achievment in other fields.

William Morris at the Kelmscott Press, advised by Emery Walker, brought about his own re-creation of the first half century of book printing. He was a medievalist with a deep love of all things Gothic, and through the books he printed he was reaching back beyond the beginnings of printing to what he saw as its roots in the beautiful illuminated manuscripts of that time, which had been written in elaborate black letter scripts. The magnificence and complexity of Kelmscott books contrast sharply with Morris's own pronouncements on how the printed page should be designed:

> I lay it down, first that a book quite unornamented can look actually and positively un-ugly, if it be so to say, architecturally good . . .
> Books whose ornament is the necessary and essential beauty which arises out of the fitness of a piece of craftsmanship for the use for which it is made.

He founded the Kelmscott Press in 1890 when he was fifty-six years old and it was the crowning achievement of his life. The printing of the Kelmscott books heralds the beginning of the third major strand in the long tradition of the private press, that of the finely printed book which is produced for its own sake. Morris succeeded in creating great works of art, but in a very different sense from William Blake. For Blake the book was a starting point, a vehicle for the artistic expression of his prophetic vision. With Morris the opposite is true, for he saw the printed and illustrated 'book beautiful' as an end in itself. He sought to create something which was self-contained—the essence of the book.

The friendship between Morris and Emery Walker, neighbours on the riverside at Hammersmith, led to Morris's decision to take up printing for himself. Emery Walker's lecture on printing at the Arts and Crafts Exhibition in London on November 15 1888 provided the catalyst Morris needed. In this lecture Walker, a printing technician of the highest order, laid down the timeless principles of good typography. An essential part of the lecture were the slides showing manuscripts and fine early printing emphasizing that good typography must be based upon sound historical principles. The importance of careful and even word spacing to avoid the white rivers of paper which run down the badly printed page was also made clear. Paper was seen to be of the essence of good printing—it must be rag based and skilfully made. The principles enunciated in this lecture provided the underlying theoretical framework for the new private press movement. In the last decade of the nineteenth century mechanisation was rampant in the printing industry, and Emery Walker understood more clearly than anyone else that what was needed was the knowledge of how best to use these new techniques.

Morris studied the craft of printing in its minutest detail. He wished to possess a typeface of his own, and his designs for the Golden type were based on the Venetian roman fount of Nicolas Jenson. Although definitely roman in origin, this heavy and dignified face leans towards the gothic. For his next types Morris returned instinctively to the gothic models and in drawing the designs for Troy and Chaucer types, which were both cut by Edward Prince, he demonstrated his close affinity with the Medieval period. For his paper Morris went to Joseph Batchelor, a paper-maker working in Ashford, Kent, who was prepared to make the experiments necessary to produce a paper which most nearly repeated the qualities of the Bolognese paper of 1473 that he regarded as the ideal. Batchelor successfully carried out his commission and all Kelmscott books were printed on paper from his mill. Morris did not undertake the printing himself: he engaged a compositor and pressmen to set his type and operate the handpress he had purchased.

The Kelmscott Press was closed in 1898, two years after Morris's death, and in the eight years of its profitable operation, 18,234 copies of fifty-three books were produced to the highest possible standards. The Kelmscott *Chaucer* is the most notable achievement of the press and the greatest artistic success of William Morris. The major contribution he made to modern book design was to conceive of each opening of a book as a unity and not merely two separate pages. Beyond this the books he printed must stand or fall upon their merits as expressions of what an artist can achieve by regarding the book itself as the receptacle of art—a thing complete in itself. The Kelmscott Press stands as a beacon lighting the way forward while not being part of the future of printing itself.

Emery Walker was the figure behind the throne at Kelmscott. Morris had offered him a partnership at the outset, but Walker declined any financial interest in the enterprise. Even so he was closely involved with Kelmscott, and Morris sought his advice before making any important decision with regard to the press. Walker also provided the essential technical underpinning for T J Cobden-Sanderson between 1900 and 1909 in their partnership at the Doves Press.

Cobden-Sanderson had come to the making of books as a binder, a craft for which he possessed great gifts. The name Doves had originally been applied to the bindery he had started in 1893. His concept of the 'book beautiful' well illustrates his own high idealism—

The Kelmscott Chaucer in facsimile, published by the Basilisk Press. Page 436 containing 'Incipit Legenda Adriane de Athenes'.

> ... the supreme Book Beautiful or Ideal Book, a dream, a symbol of the infinitely beautiful in which all things of beauty rest and into which all things of beauty do ultimately merge.

The Doves Press is the most important of the great private presses after Kelmscott, and the simplicity and absolute clarity of the pages of books printed by Cobden-Sanderson make them the most appropriate vehicles for an author's text since the Renaissance. The Doves Bible in five volumes was the greatest book from the press. In the words of Holbrook Jackson

> there is nothing, for instance, quite so effective as the first page of the Doves Bible, with its great red initial 'I' dominating the left-hand margin of the opening chapter of Genesis like a symbol of the eternal wisdom and simplicity of the wonderful Book. Neither foliation nor arabesque could better have introduced the first verse of the Creation than this flaming, sword-like initial. This edition of the Bible in itself represents the last refuge of the complex in the simple . . . .

The books from the Doves Press point the way forward and are the source of much that is fine in twentieth century book design. They were perfect from the beginning and show no signs of development, for like the many excellent books of the fifteenth century their perfection derived from an instinctive understanding on the part of the printer of the purpose of text in the book. In Cobden-Sanderson's own statement, 'the whole duty of typography is to communicate to the imagination, without loss by the way, the thought or image intended to be conveyed by the author'. His 'Ideal Book' was so clearly imagined prior to its design and execution that it was fully realized with the appearance of *Agricola* (January 1901), the first book from the press.

Cobden-Sanderson's proprietary typeface, the Doves type, was a revived version of Jenson's roman. To prepare himself for the task of design he enrolled for Edward Johnston's classes in lettering at the Central School of Arts and Crafts. The letters from his designs were re-drawn by one of Emery Walker's employees, supervised by Cobden-Sanderson. The punches were cut by E P Prince. The resulting type is a further element in the work done by the Doves Press which points the way forward to the clean and unencumbered printed pages produced by the best of contemporary private and commercial printers today. Some fifty books were issued by the press before it closed in 1916. No one else was able to benefit from employing the Doves type in their books, for starting in 1913 by disposing of the punches, Cobden-Sanderson dropped the entire stock of type into the Thames from Hammersmith Bridge. He did this despite an agreement with Emery Walker that whoever survived the other would be owner of the type. Cobden-Sanderson's monomania ensured that no one would be able to emulate him.

Third in the great triumvirate of English private presses, the Ashendene Press of C H St John Hornby, was the only one to survive the first world war. St John Hornby had founded his press in 1894 when aged twenty-seven. He had recently joined W H Smith & Son, the bookseller and stationer, eventually becoming senior partner in the firm. Daniel and his press at Oxford briefly influenced him, but early in 1895 he came under the spell of Morris. At the suggestion of Sydney Cockerell, the designs Morris had based on the Subiaco type of Sweynheym and Pannartz but never used himself, became the basis of St John Hornby's proprietary typeface. Once again Edward Prince cut the punches, producing an excellent interpretation of Morris's preliminary work. The Ashendene Subiaco type was an imposing face half-way between gothic and roman, strong and black and very beautiful, but it is hard to imagine it being used in book work today. The type first appeared in *Lo inferno di Dante* (1902) and continued in use at the press for the next twenty-five years. The Ashendene style was restrained and more influenced by the Renaissance than by things medieval. Cockerell and Emery Walker were St John Hornby's principal advisers and their friendship lasted for more than thirty years. About Walker, St John Hornby wrote in 1935 that he was 'a mine from which to draw a wealth of counsel, ever at the free disposal of any struggling beginner'.

The press was closed in 1935, and although it had been the delight and diversion of a wealthy man it was no less worthy of respect. The final publication, the *Ashendene Press Bibliography* was extensively illustrated with specimen pages from the books produced by St John Hornby, and in the words of Sydney Cockerell it was 'perfect . . . as an example of printing and compilation'. St John Hornby, writing earlier about what the press meant to him, referred to it as 'a wonderful relaxation . . . from all the cares of life and business worries'.

The three great private presses, and the Golden Cockerel Press which followed them, each owed a great debt to their compositors and press men. For, without their skill and craftsmanship and the attention they gave to every detail, the books of their respective employers would have been very ordinary.

In 1920 Harold Midgely Taylor founded the Golden Cockerel Press at Waltham St Lawrence, Berkshire. His intention was to print and publish the work of literary merit by promising young authors on a co-operative basis. Unfortunately his authors, including Martin Armstrong and

A E Coppard, did not relish the hard work involved in printing and binding books. Before very long they had all deserted their benefactor, and Taylor and his wife were left to carry on alone. After this experience a compositor and pressmen were engaged and a new policy introduced of printing fine editions of established classics. Early in 1924 Taylor's health began to deteriorate and he was obliged to sell the press to Robert Gibbings. Under the direction of its new owner, a founder member of the Society of Wood Engravers, the Press became the driving force of a new flowering of English wood engraving. Every book published between 1924 and 1933, when Gibbings sold the Golden Cockerel, contained wood engravings. The best engravers of the period were commissioned to illustrate books from the press including apart from Gibbings himself, Eric Gill, John Nash and John Farleigh. The best books from the press—*Troilus and Creseyde* (1927), *Canterbury Tales* (1929) in 4 volumes and the *Four Gospels* (1931)—also contained the finest examples of wood engraving by Gill.

The depression affected the press badly, people were no longer able to afford such magnificent books, and it was taken over in 1933 by Christopher Sandford, Owen Rutter and Francis Newbury. The Golden Cockerel typeface which had been designed by Eric Gill in 1931 continued to be used by the press even though Sandford, who acted as sole executive director, had to sell all the equipment and dismiss the craftsmen printers. By employing the commercial Chiswick Press to print his books Sandford continued to produce fine books illustrated with beautiful wood engravings throughout the 1930s.

The last private press to be considered here before passing on to the post-war period is the Perpetua Press founded by David Bland and Vivian Ridler at Bristol in 1931. In the direct line from Daniel and the Victorian parlour printers, this press also had much in common with many of the later presses, which were to be started in the 1950s. Beginning with an Adana, Bland and Ridler soon moved on to a second-hand Cropper Charlton treadle platen press which they bought for £12. Their typefaces were Baskerville and the then recently designed Perpetua of Eric Gill, from which the press took its name. In 1931 they began printing small books and the parish magazine for David Bland's father, who was the local vicar. The books they printed were often written by local authors and were distributed by James Stevens Cox, owner of the Coleridge Bookshop in Bristol. *Fifteen old nursery rhymes* with hand coloured linocuts by Biddy Darlow was selected as one of the *Fifty books of the year* in 1935. 150 copies were printed and sold by Bumpus.

In 1936 they issued what was probably their best book *The Little Chimney Sweep*, by Eric Walter White with silhouettes by Lotte Reiniger taken from her film of the same name. By now they had acquired a further press, a double-demy two-revolution cylinder press which needed a 2hp electric motor to drive it. There was only a five amp circuit in the vicarage so they had to strengthen the fuse with a nail, and every time they operated the press the local street lamps were dimmed. According to Bland however, no one seemed to notice this and they were left undisturbed. The press had been a spare time occupation for both of them so that when Vivian Ridler was offered a job by Oxford University Press in 1937, and within a month David Bland had joined Faber & Faber, the equipment had to be sold and the press closed. But one thing was certain: two young men who were later to reach the top of their chosen professions had served a very unconventional apprenticeship at their own press and had derived a great deal of enjoyment along the way.

Chapter two

SURVIVAL AND REVIVAL

The depression in the 1930s had destroyed the market for expensive books from the private presses and the second world war finally put an end to any possibility there might have been for reviving private printing on the scale and style of the Kelmscott and Doves presses. Only the Golden Cockerel remained, much changed after continuing to produce books throughout the war years. The connection with the Chiswick Press, of which Christopher Sandford was a director, had continued and in the immediate post-war period a number of handsome books were produced. Among these was Keats's *Endymion* (1947), containing sixty wood engravings by John Buckland-Wright that are probably his finest book illustrations. Later, in 1954, John Barclay's Euphormio's *Satyricon* was published in an excellent edition, but time was running out and a little later the folio *Songs and Sonnets* of John Dryden, the last book to be set in Golden Cockerel type, was one of the last attempts to revive the market for private press books in the grand manner. The press was sold in 1959 to Thomas Yoseloff, a New York publisher. Books in production were finished but nothing new came from the press. More than two hundred books had been published in the forty years of its existence and some of the best wood engraving of the twentieth century had appeared in its pages. The movement Morris had started was faltering and a new impetus was needed, though where this might come from was uncertain.

The great presses had not been able to survive in a harsh economic climate but a few artists and individualists following their own paths had managed to come through this difficult time. Several of these printers who had been making books for many years before the second world war and who would continue to do so for many years afterwards are worthy of consideration here. They were all drawing on whatever they found useful in the main private press tradition—or ignoring much of it just as they saw fit. Essentially these men were pursuing their own vision with determination and vigour. In the words of Christopher Sandford 'The private pressman today is usually by nature an artist, a Bohemian, or a rebel against convention, ideology and restraint'.

Although the foregoing description would not be wholly applicable to Fairfax Hall, this is not to his disadvantage, for he has survived as an active printer since 1930 in both England and South Africa. He is unusual in having trained himself to be his own pressman, photographer, lithographer, plate-maker, typecaster and compositor. The Stourton Press is still producing work of a very high standard in the 1970s.

It was after he had seen some books from the Ashendene Press that Fairfax Hall 'became entranced with the idea of planning and printing a book'. When he started he had no knowledge of the craft of printing. The firm he worked for let him use a spare room on their premises, where he installed a second hand press, a Cropper, and bought some Caslon type to print his first book, *All for love* by Dryden. Needless to say he ran into all kinds of trouble, and after many unsuccessful attempts it seemed as if he would never be able to print a clean sheet. Fortunately he was able to obtain the services of H Gage-Cole, who had been a pressman at Kelmscott and Doves. A very careful and thorough craftsman, Gage-Cole worked slowly and eventually *All for love* was printed successfully. Fairfax Hall, who was eager to learn all he could about hand printing, found it very difficult to prise information out of the old pressman, but he persisted and gradually improved his knowledge and skill.

The culmination of this early period came in 1934 with the production of the substantial *Catalogue of Chinese pottery and porcelain in the collection of Sir Percival David, Bt.* The Aries typeface was specially designed for this book by Eric Gill. Sir Percival David himself generously paid for all the punches, matrices and typecasting, giving everything to Hall on the understanding that the *Catalogue* would be the first book to be printed in the new type. Henceforward Aries became the proprietary typeface of the Stourton Press. It was at about the time of the publication of this book that Hall released Gage-Cole to work for St John Hornby, whose own pressman had fallen ill. Never again did Hall engage anyone to print for him. In future he was to do most of the work himself, aided only by his wife and a few friends.

He moved to South Africa in 1949 where he continued printing, returning to England in 1961 and re-establishing his press in a mews cottage near the Albert Hall. He installed a Vandercook Universal III flat bed cylinder proofing press, along with casting equipment brought from Africa. Since 1947 he had been printing a series of the works of Gurdjieff and Ouspensky. More recently he changed course again and in 1972 he printed *Pavane for a Dead Infanta*, a play by Hugh Ross Williamson, following this in 1976 with a novel, *Edwardian Romance* by Basil Creighton. He occasionally prints poems or stories of his own, the most recent of these being short stories, *Last Days* (1975). The output of the Stourton Press has been substantial and Fairfax Hall has followed his own inclinations, altering direction whenever he felt it was necessary. Throughout he has remained very much his own man.

Beginning in 1899, three years after the death of William Morris, James Guthrie followed his own path at the Pear Tree Press as an artist of the hand-press until he died in October 1952 aged seventy-eight. In the final months before he died he was working in his cottage at Flansham, Sussex, on what would have been his greatest book, a hand-coloured version of William Blake's *Songs of Innocence*. While engaged in printing this work he sprained his wrist, and his failing strength allowed him to complete only seventeen copies out of the projected edition of 200. He owed nothing to the tradition of Kelmscott and Doves. He wrote of Morris: 'great though he was, [he] is rather the figure of a tremendous amateur than of real significance as a craftsman.' Guthrie acknowledged William Blake as his true master. 'After all, we must look to the one great master—William Blake—who is the source of so much besides.'

Essayist, poet, painter and printer, Guthrie was not of the first rank, but was an original and genuine artist. His first venture, a journal called *The Elf*, contains poems with such titles as 'The Moon Fairies', 'The Changeling' and 'The Glow-Worm's Light'. This, along with some other aspects of his work, shows Guthrie merely pursuing his own idiosyncrasies, but where he demonstrates real originality is in what he called plate books. It was here that the influence of Blake was strongest. Blake's etched calligraphy and hand-coloured decoration were much more important to him than were the classical rules of typography taught by Emery Walker. The essential medium of Guthrie's most interesting work was the photographic plate. Colin Franklin writes about how

> He learnt the pleasure of writing and decorating, as one activity, then colouring the process block for each print —making every page different from the next, and from the same page in each other copy of the edition.

There was no multiplication of copies at the Pear Tree Press. Each one was unique, and some of them are among the most beautiful books of the twentieth century. His best plate book was *Frescoes from buried temples* (1928), and the rarest is the final work, the folio *Songs of Innocence*, which bears the date 1939, although he was still working on it at the time of his death. The work of James Guthrie, like that of many other artists who employ the hand-press to realize their artistic vision, is self-contained and though influenced by other artists, notably William Blake, it remains splendidly isolated.

Born in 1892 in a cottage at Harpenden, Ralph Chubb was the youngest of five children, having three sisters and a brother. A beautiful child as well as being the youngest, he seems to have belonged to a very loving family. It must have been a terrifying and unimaginable experience for him, as for so many others, when he enlisted in the army in 1914, to be sent to the trenches to fight in appalling conditions. He received a commission as a result of his Cadet Force record and was leading a platoon in France in 1915. He was later mentioned in dispatches, and in 1918 he was invalided out of the army with the rank of Captain. A grant from the army enabled him to enroll for a three-year course at the Slade. He never settled in central London and longed to return to the countryside as he had known it in childhood. It was during this time that he first discovered William Blake and was inspired to imitate and even excel the great artist-poet. Upon completion of his course he was glad to return to the family home, which had moved some years earlier to Curridge, not far from Newbury in Berkshire. Life at 'Larchwood' was much more agreeable and he became absorbed in natural things. Slowly he developed a mystical vision not unlike that of Blake. The family moved again in 1927 to Fair Oak Cottage at Ashford Hill and it was here that Chubb's best work was produced between 1933 and 1960. In his prospectus, *My path* (1932), he writes:

> Blake faced with an almost identical problem solved it in almost the same way. I accept his tradition, and am grateful, and own my obligation: still, I am no copier nor follower. Rather I take up the thread where he left it and develop the plan . . . .

Chubb produced eight lithographed volumes in the time remaining to him and it is by these that he will be judged as an artist. The first four were miscellanies: *The Sun Spirit*, *The Heavenly Cupid*, *Water Cherubs* and *The Secret Country*. Two others were volumes of tales from his childhood, *Treassure Trove* and *The Golden City*. However his masterpieces were *The Child of Dawn* and *Flames of Sunrise*. His method of production was extremely painstaking and the labour involved beyond the reach of most artists. Every word was written by hand, transferred to the stone and then hand-lithographed on the paper. In some books there are elaborate illustrations on every page and each book took years to complete. An edition of these books never amounted to more than three dozen copies, of which six would be set aside for hand colouring. With each succeeding work his mysticism deepened and this was echoed by the hand-painted pictures in the major works, which shine from the page like jewels.

His sisters continued to care for him throughout his life. They had to support him, for none of his works sold and he was never able to make any money. Towards the end of his life the cottage was full of unsold books and paintings which he was determined should be saved for posterity. To this end he sent the paintings to art galleries throughout England, and presented his books to twenty major libraries. He died on January 14 1960 and was buried at Kingsclere Woodlands Church beside his parents. At first the grave was nameless, as he had foretold, but later a stone was erected, bearing his own epitaph—

RALPH NICHOLAS CHUBB
POET AND ARTIST
'Jerusalem is built as a city
that is at unity with itself'

Wladislas V of Poland, Count Potocki of Montalk, does not fit into any tradition or classification. He is a unique personality who has flitted through the annals of the private press, living as a discontented Polish emigré for more than forty years, although he came from New Zealand, never settling anywhere for very long, and leaving behind him a trail of the most atrocious printing imaginable. He is polished, charming, a brilliant conversationalist with a biting wit, and possesses a mind which, as Rigby Graham writes, is 'viciously incisive'. In the 1930s he suffered imprisonment for obscenity, despite financial and moral support from such public figures as Aldous Huxley, H G Wells, J B Priestley and T S Eliot. In 1936 he bought a small proto-Adana press to print the first issue of his journal the *Right Review*, and in the following eleven years published seventeen issues, in the course of which he overcame almost insuperable difficulties, including the confiscation of his press and papers by the British authorities after the fall of France.

He was never concerned with the typographical niceties, and in the foreword to *Music Within Me* wrote

> ... the French who, unlike the English, have too much sense to judge a poem by the price of the printing machine used to print it, at once responded with the most glowing praises of the translations ...

Potocki travelled to Bari in Italy in August 1948 and on his return sold his printing equipment. He then emigrated to Draguignan in France, only to return once again, to Dorset, in the early 1960s where he settled at Lovelace's Copse between Piddletrenthide and Haslebury Bryan with his daughter and a miscellaneous collection of animals. This temporary home, described by Rigby Graham as 'a long low building of the kind used for deep litter chicken houses' was where he had established the Melissa Press. He used an old demi-folio treadle press, setting his type quickly and carelessly which caused the occasional letter in the wrong fount to appear in a word. His respect for language, however, was much greater and he took care to ensure that no literals appeared in the final text.

Late in the 1960s Potocki returned to Draguignan where he continued printing. He has moved frequently between England and France during the past decade. Occasionally he has had pieces printed for him by other printers. David Chambers produced a cycle of love poems, *Meillerie* (1972), with an engraving by Mark Severin. The Melissa Press is still active in Draguignan and its work continues to be recorded by David Chambers in the annual volumes of *Private Press Books*.

Guido Morris inhabited a completely different world from Potocki. While the Count appeared to be aristocratic in lineage and bearing, although typographically somewhat underdeveloped, Morris came from the bourgeoisie, was withdrawn, at times almost monk-like, and had set his heart on the search for perfection in the craft of printing. They met in a rather prickly encounter in the British Museum Reading Room, and Potocki was not impressed. He later expressed his doubts about the quality of Morris's work, referring to his 'purrfect printing'. On the cover of one of the exhibition catalogues he printed, Guido Morris states his own belief in the following advertisement:

GUIDO MORRIS, ARCHITYPOGRAPHUS.

There can be no gainsaying his ideal, yet he seemed to lack

consistency and the intensity of purpose necessary to the achievement of his objective.

In 1946 he re-opened the Latin Press, for the seventh time in its chequered career, at St Ives, on the Wastrel in the old part of the town. The Latin Press had first been established in Langford, Somerset in 1935, while Morris was still employed by Bristol Zoo. His intention had been to print a broadsheet magazine for his employer, and he managed to produce four before his job came to an end. At this time he knew nothing about printing, but he received excellent advice from Eric Gill, Beatrice Warde, and John Johnson, printer at the Oxford University Press. His design and execution improved steadily under their guidance, and after leaving Bristol to work at his press in Langford he was able to attract a steady stream of commissions. Unfortunately he was unpredictable and seemed unable to keep to deadlines—an unforgivable sin for a jobbing printer, as he now styled himself—and custom fell away. Beatrice Warde provided him with money at first but she soon had to withdraw when the bills became too large. This irresponsibility was to spoil his career. He could have been one of the best printers in England, but he was always letting his patrons down.

Becoming even more unsettled he moved from place to place, from Somerset to London, then, after living for a while in Northampton, to Cornwall just before the outbreak of war, but there was nowhere he could settle down and take up the work for which he was best suited. When war intervened the Latin Press was closed. Throughout his wartime service he occupied himself with the obsessive compilation of an enormous Latin dictionary which he had no hope of completing. At the same time he was studying Hebrew under the guidance of a sympathetic officer. His reason for doing this was, at least in part, to be able to realize his ideal of an abstract typography to be enjoyed by those who saw it simply

ON PRINTING BY HAND

Hand-printing is a craft to be enjoyed for itself as well as for the satisfaction that is to be had from the production of books and pamphlets that may in turn please others. It is a slow pursuit, the more so if perfection in content, in layout, and impression are sought after; but this quest, despite its certain failure, adds much to the pleasure of handling type, ink, paper and presses.

The quality of the text is more important than that of the printing, but the selection of suitable material, other than poetry, is not easy. I have inclined, myself, towards notes on printing history, the careful proofing of wood-engravings, and a scattering of experimental work.

Book production at the Cuckoo Hill Press has been so slow that it has seemed sensible to use the finest materials available. I have founts of Romanée, Bembo, Fournier and Modern, as well as small quantities of various decorative faces; for books with much text, however, I have had the type

AT THE CUCKOO HILL PRESS

machine-set, getting a greater variety of faces and a sharper impression from the new metal. Ink applied with a hand-roller needs to be very stiff, and for many years I have used a Coates lithographic ink, with added driers. The paper has usually been hand-made: damped European for type and for strongly cut engravings, Japanese for more delicate work. A demy folio Alexandra Albion press, made in 1884, has been used for most of my pieces: accurately adjusted, with a new tympan for each job, and with the help of a number of type-high bearers, it has printed easily and well.

Pamphlets have normally been sewn and put into paper wrappers at the press. It has however been difficult to get completely satisfactory cases from the trade at a price which is suitable for the slight extent of most of my books, though some made recently by Cambridge University Press for a reproduction of Fournier le jeune's small type-specimen book were very successful.   April 1977

On printing by hand, written and printed by David Chambers, Cuckoo Hill Press. Opening containing text.

for its beauty of design, with no reference to its meaning. This overriding concern for design at the expense of everything else, even his jobbing work, illustrates one of the major reasons for his inability to maintain solvency.

After the war, when he returned to St Ives, he had a completely new start and full support from friends in the artists colony, as well as from local people. He produced the usual range of jobbing printing—letterheads, exhibition catalogues, posters and similar items, and a number of small books including the 'Crescendo Poetry' series. Larger books, including *Letters of Fr. Rolfe Baron Corvo to Grant Richards* for the bookseller George Sims, and *Treasures of a London Temple*, a study of the plate at Bevis Marks, were produced for commercial publishers. These books were too large for Morris to print himself, so he had them machined from type he had set by Kenneth Worden in Marazion, only a few miles from St Ives. But as he sold his books and jobbing work too cheaply, he earned nothing like an adequate wage. According to Cave 'His printing had a splendid monumental quality, seen at its best in some of his broad-sheets and letters to such friends as Gordon Craig—which he used to set up in type and print a single copy . . . '

He was a good printer but he seemed to lack business sense and he was constantly finding himself in financial difficulty. From time to time he would let his customers down badly and this sort of thing did nothing to encourage new business. The orders began to fall away and he was faced with bankruptcy. Worden, in Marazion, claimed his Albion press and type in settlement of outstanding debts. The future looked bleak and finally Guido Morris gave in, left St Ives, and joined London Transport, becoming a guard on the Underground railway. Rumours circulated for some time that he would be returning to printing, which he seems to have done briefly in the late 1960s and early 1970s. He printed a few poetry leaflets, but unfortunately nothing substantial. Eventually even these ceased to appear, and the private press movement was deprived of one of its more colourful personalities.

Morris survived for a long time, fighting to overcome personal difficulties, but despite repeated attempts by friends and sympathetic patrons to help him he failed in the end to help himself. Comparisons are odious, but it is now necessary to turn to the revival of printing in the post-war period and examine the career of a jobbing printer who was successful. Will Carter, who established the Rampant Lions Press in Cambridge in 1949, was everything that poor Morris was not. He possessed sound business judgement and had undergone long training in calligraphy and printing before finally setting himself up as a one man printing practice. Will Carter had become interested in printing when he was twelve years old and his first press had been a small Adana. From the beginning he seemed to have an intuitive appreciation of design and his skill developed quickly. On leaving school he was offered a job for two years with Unwin Brothers at Woking, learning everything he could about all aspects of printing from composition through machining and binding to office work.

He began to print books when he moved to a small flat in Cambridge in 1934. A chance meeting with the poet Robert Nichols led to a commission for printing three poems, *A Spanish Triptych*. Realizing that he would not be able to do justice to the work on his Adana, he borrowed money to purchase an Albion, taught himself how to use it and went on to print several more small books in the following months. By now he was working for Heffers, printers and publishers in Cambridge, so his day-time work was complementing his spare time avocation. More jobbing work was coming his way and his reputation was steadily growing. Interest in calligraphy and graphic design led him to visit the workshop of the late Rudolf Koch in Frankfurt, where he first met Herman Zapf. Zapf was to have a considerable influence on Carter, and this is evident from the latter's typeface, Klang. Carter served in the Royal Navy during the war, returning to take up his work with Heffers again in 1946.

Unsettled by the return to civilian life he began to think very seriously about becoming his own master. In the anniversary volume, *The First Ten* (1959), he wrote :

> I was convinced that there was a market for fine jobbing printing of the sort that was too small to be handled by big printing houses and yet was beyond the scope of the small jobbing firm.

Once the decision had been made, he left Heffers and set to work on his own account.

An Autovic platen press was acquired in 1950 and printing from the Rampant Lions began developing those hallmarks of faultless impression and superb inking for which it is internationally renowned. In these early years two typefaces predominated: Bembo, an old face, and a modern one, Times New Roman. Today Carter's Octavian and Zapf's Palatino have come into their own, both in jobbing work and for books. A recent book from the press, *Areopagitica* by John Milton, has been most elegantly printed in Palatino. Carter's instinctive grasp of the principles of good design is illustrated by his comment:

> It's a little bit frightening that some of my early customers and even printers I've known can't tell the difference between good and bad design. All I can say after these many years is that the subject and the way of its application has become a mania and a conviction and can't be taught at all.

While he was working on his own it was inevitable that as the demand for his services grew there would be a move away from jobbing towards more interesting book work and this was certainly apparent by the end of the 1950s. However when Will Carter was joined by his son Sebastian in the early 1960s it was possible once again for the Rampant Lions Press to undertake such commissions for selected clients.

Since 1963 however it has been in book printing that the press has displayed its maturity and complete mastery. This has been most evident in the Clover Hill Editions produced in collaboration with Douglas Cleverdon and Louis Cowan, owner of the Chilmark Press in New York. The first was *The Ancient Mariner* (1963) with an introduction by David Jones. The triumvirate were very interested in producing poetry by contemporary poets, and in 1967 the second book to appear in the series was *The Elegies of a Glass Adonis* by Constantine Trypanis.

After the seventh Clover Hill book had appeared Louis Cowan withdrew because most of the authors in the series were not well known in the USA. His place was taken by Sebastian Carter and the programme has continued successfully throughout the 1970s. The achievement of Will Carter, single handed at first and later with his son, has been twofold: on the one hand to reach a standard of jobbing printing never before attained in England, and on the other to print limited editions of books which bear comparison with the best that are being produced anywhere in the world today. This has been done, not as William Morris did, by designing books for others to print, but by an artist-craftsman working alone designing books with meticulous care and printing with consummate skill. Will Carter is the dominant figure in English private printing since 1945 and anyone who wants to produce fine books that really belong to the late twentieth century must take account of his work and absorb what it can teach them.

Many books produced by private printers are very expensive, putting them beyond the reach of many people. Recognizing this, Charles Ede founded the Folio Society in 1947 'to produce editions of the world's great literature in a format worthy of the contents, at a price within the reach of everyman'. The first home of the society was provided in an attic in Soho by the binders Sangorski & Sutcliffe. From the beginning a policy of providing a balanced annual programme was established. During the year a new title was published each month and members had to purchase at least four of them, at an annual cost in the early 1950s of £3 10s. Works of fiction, history, poetry, drama and memoirs were carefully selected and edited for each annual programme. New books not previously published were included, such as *The Trial of Joan of Arc* which contained verbatim reports from the ecclesiastical courtroom. Illustrations were included in nearly all the society's books, and artists such as Michael Ayrton, John Bratby, Joan Hassall, Garrick Palmer and John Piper were commissioned for such work. Everything possible was done to ensure that the style of the artist selected harmonized with that of the author.

Within ten years of its foundation the membership of the society had exceeded five figures, enabling initial print-runs of 10,000 copies to be placed for some titles, a situation many commercial publishers would envy. Such relatively large editions have contributed to keeping prices to members more or less in line with those in the open market. The Folio Society, which is still flourishing today, contributed a great deal to the revival of fine printing in the first decade after the second world war by bringing first class literary texts embodied in superbly designed books within the reach of thousands of ordinary people.

One of the valuable services performed by private presses is that of discovering the special subject field, where an unsatisfied demand exists for well-produced books in editions too small in number to interest a commercial publisher. This was the point of departure for Raymond Lister who established The Golden Head Press in 1952. Previously he had experimented by issuing, in collaboration with R I Stevens Ltd, a Cambridge printer, *A title list of books on minature painting* in an edition of sixty copies, of which fifty were for sale, selling them all within a few weeks of publication. This set the pattern of book production for the press. Raymond Lister commissioned and designed his books and then used the services of commercial firms to print and bind them. The first Golden Head book was *A bibliography of the first editions of Philip Henry Gosse FRS*, with introductory essays by Sacheverell Sitwell and Geoffrey Lapage. Other books followed and those containing essays of limited interested were interspersed with Lister's own visionary writings. By the early 1960s there was a stock list of twenty-eight titles and the Golden Head Press was well established with its own idiosyncratic niche in private printing.

John Peters and Peter Foster deliberately set out to revive the pre-war standards of private press book production. The Vine Press of Hemingford Grey, Huntingdon, though a leisurely operation, was intended to make books that would stand beside the great work of Kelmscott and Doves. Operations began in October 1956. *Vitis Vera*, an anthology of verses from the Vulgate and Authorized versions of the Bible with an introduction recalling the re-introduction of viticulture at Hemingford Grey and Godmanchester, was published in 1957 in an edition of forty copies which were mostly presented to friends of the pressmen.

With this preliminary exercise behind them the partners set out to produce the work of contemporary authors in fine limited editions. Gradually they gained experience and mastered their old Imperial press which had been made c1860 by Cope and Sherwin. Throughout their labours they continued to do all they could to emulate the work of the best hand-press printers. Using hand rollers for inking they were able to print several colours at once on the carefully damped hand-made paper which was used for all but one of their books. Their most ambitious work was *The Parliament of Women*, a poetic drama in three acts by Sir Herbert Read. The text was set in 16 point Monotype Centaur with three colour illustrations by Reg Boulton, combining end-grain engraving, linocuts and relief-etched plates. Work began early in 1959 but such were the complications in printing the book that it was not completed until late in the following year. The last book to come from the press, *Twenty-five poems* by Evelyn Ansell with wood engravings by Diana Bloomfield, was printed on what was probably the last of the paper made by J Batchelor for William Morris. Printing on the dampened paper was successfully completed but the sheets needed interleaving before binding to avoid offset. Unfortunately the trade binder put the folded sheets in a hydraulic press without interleaving with disastrous results. Only ten copies which had been sent for binding in full leather, and not treated in this way, satisfied the printers that they had reached 'the limit in presswork of what we felt we could achieve with our archaic equipment'.

This done they called a halt to their printing at the end of 1963 having proved that operating a private press to the highest possible standard did not require private means. After payment had been made to authors, artists and suppliers, there had always been adequate funds remaining to furnish one bottle of claret for each shift—a most appropriate and gratifying reward for all their labours.

Chapter three

A NEW MOVEMENT

While The Vine Press was sustaining its spirited revival of the ideals of Kelmscott and Doves, a new variety of private press was beginning to make its way in the world. Cave refers to its emergence as 'a remarkable revival of the parlour printers'.

This reference to middle-class family printing in the nineteenth century is apt, for these mid-twentieth century private printers owed more to C H O Daniel than to the movement initiated by William Morris. The new movement was not inspired by ideals of self-enlightenment but was seeking ways of learning craft skills as a relief from the increasing flood of mass produced goods and services. Although many presses made books and pamphlets which were then exchanged for those produced by others similarly engaged, there were the beginnings of a market appearing and sales were being made to customers, mainly through mailing lists. On the practical level the presses were no longer being housed in the parlour—modern homes are not so spacious as were their counterparts in Victorian times—but in garages, cellars or sheds in gardens.

This burgeoning interest in the art of printing was quickened and propagated with the publication of John Ryder's *Printing for pleasure* Phoenix House, 1955. It was a short practical manual that was both scholarly and comprehensive without being dull, full of enthusiasm for the art of amateur printing. Ryder himself was a typographer with Phoenix House and in his spare time a private printer using his own 'Miniature Press' for experimental work. He did not produce very much, but his attractive *Suite of Fleurons* Phoenix

House, 1956, was a virtuoso exercise that added to his influence, encouraging amateur printers to improve their own typography. *Printing for pleasure* became so popular that another edition was made available in 1957 by the English Universities Press in their 'Teach Yourself' series. A large number of private printers collaborated in a very interesting venture when Thomas Rae and Geoffrey Handley-Taylor solicited their help in compiling *The book of the private press* Signet Press, 1958, an international directory of private presses. This was a basic reference work and it is a great pity that there has been only the one edition. More than 240 amateur printers were listed and information was given about names and addresses, dates of establishment, makes of presses and typeface used. An indication was also given of the principal publications of each press, and the type of press was defined according to John Ryder's classification. Inevitably incomplete because of the difficulties of gathering information by questionnaire, it was nonetheless an invaluable reference tool.

Another of Ryder's contributions to furthering the cause of the private press movement was the *Minature folio of private presses* (1960) in which he gathered together printed specimens of the work of twenty-eight presses. Each one consisted of four pages measuring 6½ x 4½ inches, and the collection was loosely gathered into a folder with a printed reproduction of an old engraving of a printing shop on the front cover. Of the twenty-eight presses only six had been working before 1950, sixteen came from Great Britain, nine from the USA and one each from Holland, Italy, and Germany. Apart from providing a means of presenting the work of the presses to a wider audience Ryder was also wanting to make some assessment of the abilities of the printers involved:

This assessment will be measured on a printer's ability to use type in a functional way (plus interest, and decoration as it comes naturally to him) ...

His critical notes were published in *Book design and production*, Autumn 1962. One hundred sets were printed, the printers themselves receiving one each, the remainder being distributed free to persons prominent in the world of fine printing.

Some part-time printers were seeking to improve their skills by joining appropriate societies. The Amateur Printers Association had been founded as early as 1944 by a Bristol printer, William R Brace, to bring together all those who were interested in printing. Brace wanted to create an organisation which would allow printers to exchange experiences, pass on hints and tips, and promote the spirit of craftsmanship. In 1948 its name was changed to the International Small Printers Association; subsequently there was a second change and ISPA became the British Printing Society in 1965. There are now over eight hundred members governed by an elected executive council of unpaid officers. According to Kenneth Hardacre, a former president of the society, about one quarter of the membership are private printers while the majority run their own print shops or small commercial publishing businesses, and for them this society performs the functions of a trade association. It is a mixed body of people interested in printing for a variety of reasons, but it has proved a very useful forum for those of its members who only print for their own delight.

The Private Libraries Association, founded in 1956 as an international society of book collectors, had among its founding membership an enthusiastic minority who were closely involved in private printing. In 1959 the Society of Private Printers was set up, under the auspices of the PLA, as an informal group of private printers intending to collaborate through an exchange of ideas and printed specimens. Exchanges of correspondence and visits continue to take place and information on printing techniques has regularly been exchanged between members. Occasionally arrangements have also been made for the disposal of unwanted equipment. Recently members, of whom there are about fifty, have combined to produce miniature folios on common themes. The most recent one to be completed was, like Ryder's *Miniature folio*, a series of specimens identifying the presses of members and including photographs of themselves and their print shops. Currently they are attempting to produce another miniature folio, this time of children's books. This is proving quite difficult and David Chambers, honorary publications secretary of the PLA, who is coordinating the project, is finding that it is taking a long time to obtain the necessary number of contributions.

An even more informal association of private printers was established in 1962. The London Chappel had no more than a dozen members at its foundation including Kenneth Hardacre (Kit-Cat Press), Paul Peter Piech (Taurus Press) and James Mosley (Martindale Press and librarian at St Bride Printing Library). They co-operated in a number of exhibitions in the following years but the Chappel became basically a dining club and of late only a fond memory, although Kenneth Hardacre retains his interest in it and feels it ought to be revived.

Several new journals were founded during the late 1950s and early 1960s which provided platforms for those wishing to write about private presses. The most important one, *The Private Library*, the quarterly journal of the PLA has been, since its inception in 1957, very generous with space for articles on private printing. During the past twenty years it has continued to be the main source of information about the presses and their publications. Recording the output of the private presses has always been a problem because the trade bibliographies and even the *British National Bibliography*, which started in 1950, have never been interested in such books. Occasionally a few items are listed, but seemingly by accident. The PLA was once again helpful when it decided to provide financial backing for the new annual bibliography edited by Thomas Rae and Roderick Cave, *Private press books*, which was first published in 1960, listing books issued in the western world during 1959. It has since become the most important annual bibliography of its kind published anywhere in the world.

Interest in private presses was growing rapidly towards the end of the 1950s, and in the spring of 1958 the first issue of the new quarterly journal *Book design and production*, edited by James Moran, was published. Although it was concerned with the commercial printing industry, the editor was devoted to improving the standard of its output, and in his first editorial entitled 'Raison d'etre' James Moran wrote ' . . . only the best is good enough—both in contents and the look of a book'. Further on in the same editorial he continued '*Book design and production* will do its best to encourage good design in books; it will provide a forum for discussion on technical and aesthetic problems . . . .'

A private press owner himself, Moran frequently included articles and notes on private presses in this journal and by doing so spread knowledge about the small world of the private press to a much larger audience. Moran was writing constantly about the effect of new technologies on printing, and expressing his feeling that the private presses would become repositories for the old craft skills which were being discarded and otherwise lost in the rush for ever cheaper and quicker ways of printing books. He launched 'a modest quarterly called *The Black Art*' in the spring of 1962 with a view to preserving such knowledge as was worthwhile, remarking that if the uninitiated thought that it dealt in magic he would not mind, if that helped increase circulation. The material included was generally of a historical nature but there were also a number of articles on contemporary private presses. It continued for the next three years to be scholarly, in a modest way, without being boring, serving its editor's purpose admirably.

In the USA at this time, awareness of private press practices in England was being encouraged by articles carried in the quarterly *American Book Collector*. Often the writers of these articles, devotees like Roderick Cave and Rigby Graham, were also writing for *The Private Library*. On both sides of the Atlantic the private printer was enjoying growing public interest in his work. Information was being disseminated in all manner of ways, as a consequence of the fact that there had, since the early 1950s, been a large increase in the number of people who wanted to print for themselves. This received visible expression in England in April 1961 when the Times bookshop held an exhibition of 'English private presses 1757-1961'. Included were the books of ninety-five presses from Horace Walpole's Strawberry Hill Press of the 1750s to Ben Sands's Shoestring Press of the 1950s. John Carter, brother of Will Carter, in his introduction to the catalogue of the exhibition wrote of the private press where 'the printer is more interested in making a good book than a fat profit'.

This has always been true of the owners of private presses, but a new emphasis had emerged in the 1950s which was made explicit in the title of John Ryder's *Printing for pleasure*. The accent was to be placed on enjoyment. This is in no way meant to imply that the presses were merely frivolous—far from it— but in Will Ransom's words:

The simplest and perhaps the truest type of private press is that maintained by one who is, at least by desire, a craftsman and finds a peculiar joy in handling type, ink, and paper, with sufficient means and leisure to warrant such an avocation. His literary selection may leave something to be desired and art may be disregarded or amazingly interpreted but he has a good time.

Among the owners of private presses who started printing in the 1950s and obtained a great deal of pleasure from their presses were David Chambers, a scholar printer at the Cuckoo Hill Press, Ben Sands, an artist using a hand-press at the Shoestring Press, Roy Lewis, a journalist publishing poetry from his own press at the Keepsake Press, and Kenneth Hardacre, a teacher of English Literature and fine printer at the Kit-Cat Press. All are still active in their very different ways and each one of them has by his own efforts become a skilled craftsman. Between them they have more than a century of experience of private printing and their work is examined in some detail in Part two and checklists of their publications are included in the Appendix.

One important figure in the private press movement who has already been mentioned is Thomas Rae. Although a Scot, and thus strictly outside the scope of this book, his contribution to the private press movement in England is of considerable importance and it is on this basis that his work is considered here. He was junior partner in a family firm of jobbing printers and became interested in printing books in the early 1950s. He produced an extract from *Pickwick papers* in pamphlet form, as an experiment in making Dickens readable. Feeling reasonably satisfied with this he founded the Signet Press in 1956, which he ran from his home in Greenock, Scotland. A slim pamphlet, *Thomas Bewick, wood engraver* (1956), was the first item from the new press, printed to aid an appeal for donations to the St Bride Printing Library.

In 1958, the year that he published *The book of the private press*, he also wrote and printed a short study, *Androw Myllar, Scotland's First Printer*. It was handsomely produced but so severly criticized in *The Scottish Historical Review* that Rae decided against any further essays into the realms of scholarship, although he was not altogether deterred from publishing small books on the history of printing, and in 1962 he published *Some notes on wood engraving* selected from Thomas Bewick's *Memoir* illustrated with engravings printed from the artist's original blocks. Editing *Private press books* with David Chambers and Roderick Cave was taking up a great deal of his time and after contributing to four annual volumes he gave up his part of the work because of increasing business commitments. The output from the Signet Press too began to slow down at this time. Rae was made to change the name of his press in 1967 because of its similarity to that of an American paperback series. Under its new name, Grian-aig Press, he issued *Poems* (1969) by Joan Prince and *The Ettricke garland* (1971). Some printing was done for others by Rae. In 1967 he printed W J Stannard's *Anaglyptography* for the Plough Press, Loughborough, and in the following year he produced the excellent small book *The private press: handbook to an exhibition* for Loughborough School of Librarianship. Very little has been heard from the Grain-Aig Press in the 1970s which is a pity because Rae's printing had a dignified simplicity not often seen in recent private press books. Roderick Cave described his work as

> sober, usually without any typographical fireworks . . . and depending for its effect on the clarity of the traditional layout and the sound presswork—as befits an Elder of the Kirk.

The contrasts between private printers rate highly among the delights to be derived from any study of private presses, and Kim Taylor, owner of the Ark Press, provides a nice illustration of this when contrasted with Thomas Rae. In an account of his press he relates his first experience in the printing shop.

> It was therefore the fulfilment of an old dream to stand one wintry day in 1954, within sound of the Cornish sea, in a lofty shed blackened by the herrings once smoked there, and in the company of cold type, ink, paper, and the amiable, undying monster of a century-old handpress. For a first exercise in setting I chose a passage by Kierkegaard on silence.

Taylor was only able to print a few things on his own press such as letterheads and a fine folio *St Matthew's Passion* with the entire text cut in linoleum by John Cossar, before turning to Kenneth Worden of Marazion, as Guido Morris had done before him. After his early experiments he had decided that what he wanted to do was publish interesting texts accompanied by good illustrations, and to do this at the sort of price most people could afford. The first Ark book was *Life* by D H Lawrence with wood engravings by Ru Van Rossem, priced at 7s 6d. Taylor continues to decide which texts are suitable, edit them, design and direct their production, and Kenneth Worden prints them.

Glory on Earth (1960) by D C Peattie, with wood engravings by Otto Rohse, one of the finest engravers of the twentieth century, is still available, priced £3.00. The Ark Press continues to issue excellent books at prices well below those charged by commercial publishers for similar items.

Two presses with similar specialisations which began printing in 1956 were the Allenholme Press of Peter Isaac and the

ANAGLYPTOGRAPHY
Medallion engraving for book illustration

Reprinted, with an original anaglyptograph, from the
Art Exemplar [1859] by
William John Stannard

PLOUGH PRESS
1967

Anaglyptography by W J Stannard. Printed by Thomas Rae, Grian-aig Press. Published by Geoffrey Wakeman, Plough Press. Title page.

Merrion Press of Susan Shaw . Both press owners were interested in material on typographical history, tending towards bibliography at Allenhome, while Merrion inclined towards calligraphy and English literature. Peter Isaac issued several fasicules of 'Bulmer Papers'. Susan Shaw, in contrast, decided to turn her press into a specialist commercial operation and the first Merrion Press publication in this new guise was *Wolperiana; an illustrated guide to Berthold L Wolpe, with various observations by Charles Mozley* (1960). The Merrion Press is still in business and one of its most recent publications is *The common press* (2 volumes, 1978) by Elizabeth Harris with drawings and advice on construction by Clinton Sisson. Volume one contains a description of the eighteenth century hand press housed in the Smithsonian Institution, which is supposed to have been used by Benjamin Franklin in 1726 when he was employed in the printing house of John Watts in Wild Court near Lincoln's Inn Fields, London. It is a romantic story which is very difficult to substantiate but the press is now known as the 'Franklin press'. Volume two contains eight folded sheets of plans for reconstructing the press; a task very few people would be equipped to undertake, since such blacksmith's skills as fulling and swaging are not easily acquired. The two volumes are bound in an attractive slip-case. Susan Shaw does printing of her own, and commissions work from printers and collaborates with overseas publishers such as David Godine in Boston, Massachusetts, publishing really excellent texts in attractive formats.

The borderline between private and commercial interest in the sphere of the private press is always blurred. The Merrion Press seems to be situated in this area of confusion. It began as a private press, but is now more accurately described as a small, specialist publishing house, trading commercially yet retaining considerable affinity with the private presses. This connection is worth retaining because it provides a channel through which the private press is linked to be a larger world, and in the reverse direction a source of inspiration and new ideas which might be of great value in exploiting and sustaining the open market in times of economic difficulty.

The 1950s saw the development of an important regional private press movement in Leicestershire. One centre of activity was Leicester College of Art, where John Mason, a lecturer in bookbinding, started experimenting with different ways of making paper by hand. He was the son of J H Mason who in his earlier years had been chief compositor at the Doves Press. John Mason's work with handmade paper began in his own home in 1954, when he collected some montbretia leaves and turned them into sheets of paper in a mould and deckle of his own design. At the invitation of his college principal he later transferred these activities to the college of art. Before long his students were enthusiastically combing the countryside, and even their own homes, for suitable materials for paper making. Some went further and began printing, using their own handmade paper. In a lecture given at the Double Crown Club, London, in 1967 Mason listed the plants he had used:

> Gladioli, wallflowers, michaelmas daisies, montbretia, asparagus, iris, potato, beans, and nettle stalks, cow parsley and all kinds of wild grasses became my raw material.

The papers he made took on a great variety of colour and texture, and this can be seen to good effect in the Private Libraries Association's edition of his address to the Double Crown Club, *Twelve by eight* (1959). He had succeeded in 1955 in making paper from nylon and the sheets had proved when tested to be enormously strong and resistant to the action of mould and strong chemicals. Mason thought they would be 'the ideal imperishable material for documents and records and for paper currency, for packaging of corrosive substances and who knows what else'.

Helping John Mason with practical and artistic research at this time was Rigby Graham, who produced some very interesting pictures in Mason's experimental papers with skeleton leaves and coloured threads. At the same time, a number of people who had no connection with the college of art, including Duine Campbell, Toni Savage, Boyd Lichfield, Penelope Campbell, Patricia Green, and Patricia Harris were beginning to take up printing, and Graham helped several of them establish presses. His continuing interest and great enthusiasm have led to his becoming the dominant figure in the Leicestershire private press scene.

The first press that Rigby Graham was associated with was the Orpheus Press, established in 1958 by Douglas Martin. Styling itself 'the fugitive private press' it proved to be a chaotic undertaking. At first it worked, without equipment of its own, on borrowed presses. The finest publication produced by the press was *Die Sonette an Orpheus* (1959) by Rainer Maria Rilke, printed on Mason's Twelve by Eight paper, and including twelve three-coloured lithographs by Rigby Graham. Martin was away in Germany for some time, and on his return he found a patron who was willing to put the press on a better footing. Improved premises were found and ambitious projects discussed but they never came to anything. More typical of the press was its method of distributing such pamphlets as *Kirby Hall: an uninformative guide* (1960) in the local pubs. Rigby Graham records the fate of John Clare's *Lines written in Northampton County Asylum*: 'scores were offered for next to nothing in pubs, used as beer mats, and eventually hurled at sneering crowds in the market place on Saturday morning'. The Orpheus Press never seemed capable of living up to its early promise and after two years gave up the unequal struggle and disappeared.

In 1961, after trying without success to revive the Orpheus imprint, Rigby Graham, Patricia Green and Toni Savage adopted the name Pandora and a new press emerged. They had little equipment—an Adana flat-bed press and two cases of battered type—but they produced some interesting books in small formats, such as Byron's *When we two parted*, and *Poems and translations* by Count Potocki. These were all produced for the very good reason that they wanted to print them. Most of the books from the Pandora Press had colour illustrations requiring two or three impressions, and in the most substantial book from the press, Thea Scott's *Fingal's Cave*, the fifty-two pages went through the press eighty times. After the seventy-sixth printing the sheets had been spread out over the attic floor in the old rectory at Aylestone, when a sudden spell of sunshine hatched the woodworm in the floor and more than one hundred sheets were peppered with holes. The sheets had a five colour linocut and reprinting was impossible, so the edition had to be reduced by almost half. The Pandora Press experienced financial difficulties and closed down in 1968. Rigby Graham and Toni Savage were not to be discouraged as both of them had also established their own presses.

Trevor Hickman, who bound *Fingal's Cave* for the Pandora Press, was encouraged by Graham to establish his own press in 1962. The Brewhouse Press took its name from the old brewhouse attached to Hickman's home in Wymondham where it was set up. Trained in bookbinding, he was far more interested in the binding of books from his press than are most other private press owners. The first publication from

Brewhouse was *Chidiock Tichbourne* (1964) a twelve page booklet containing the last letter and an elegy by a plotter against Queen Elizabeth I, with illustrations by Rigby Graham. A dozen copies were bound by Trevor Hickman with the spine in black morocco leather, the title blocked in gold, and the light green morocco boards with a red onlay on the front blocked in gold. Paper wrappers were used on the rest of the edition of two hundred and fifty copies. *The Pickworth Fragment* (1966) was selected for the National Book League's exhibition of book design in the same year. It was an original variation on a Japanese form of binding, in which a series of pages were joined at the fore-edges to make a panorama of text and coloured linocuts nearly fourteen feet long. Enclosed in a quarter-binding of brown suede it had gold-tooled and coloured linocuts on the brown paper boards.

The Brewhouse produced an annotated bibliography, *Camus in English* (1968), listing Albert Camus's contributions to newspapers and periodicals. In 1970 a scholarly work on Victorian printing came from the press—this was Geoffrey Wakeman's *Aspects of Victorian lithography, anastatic printing and photozincography*. Brewhouse Broadsheets were started in 1966 and altogether thirteen were published by 1974 when the series ceased publication. *The execution of a bookbinder* by Trevor Hickman was the first to appear. Broadsheets 3 and 4 were published together entitled *Silence at Midnight* and *Silence à Minuit* recording clandestine printing in France during the German occupation. Number 13, the last, gives a brief account of the history of the Brewhouse Press.

Rigby Graham, despite his involvement with other people's presses, was able to find time to establish his own Cog Press in 1963. Originally he had trained as a mural painter, but he was not to be limited to this single activity and went on to achieve some success as an illustrator, graphic designer, bookbinder and writer. He regularly contributed to a large number of private press books and little magazines in Britain and abroad. The Cog Press is experimental and grew out of Graham's interest in the PLA's Society of Private Printers. The first book he produced was *Cogs in Transition* (1963), sixty copies, printed for this society. He used an Adana Horizontal Quarto hand-press, a nipping press, and an old 'Favourite' gas-powered gold stamping press which was eventually converted to natural gas. The next book was *El Icaro* (1965) by Salvador Jacinto Polo de Medina, printed in an edition of forty copies. Several numbers of a magazine *Enigma*, devoted to literature and graphics and including essays, poems and prints by Rigby Graham and others, were issued by the press. Books have continued to come from the Cog Press while the indefatigable and prolific Graham has all the time been contributing to a wide range of books and periodicals in several countries. The press is not intended to be too serious and this is reflected in the series of broadsheets with such titles as *Pro Bono Publico* and *A rough night*, which have been given away to friends. In 1968 Graham wrote and illustrated *Slieve Bingian: a cycle of prints and drawings*, and for once he succeeded in producing a book which gave him some lasting satisfaction.

The Black Knight Press was first established in Bath in 1964 by Duine Campbell. He moved to Leicester in 1967 where Black Knight soon became a well known part of the local private press scene. The productions of the press, which are all well printed, have usually been small books in limited editions on Japanese or English hand-made papers.

William Blake is very important to Campbell and he has produced a series of books employing his own illustrations to accompany texts taken from the poet's works. They have included *A Divine Image* (1968), *Infant Sorrow* (1970), and

Proverbs of Hell (1972). A more ambitious project completed by Black Knight was *The Rubaiyat of Omar Khayyam* where each page was printed separately and more than 25,000 impressions were required to complete the printing. Such was the interest in this excellent book that in 1977 it was reprinted by photolithography for the Kingsmead Press in Bath.

Leicestershire continues to be a good place for private presses to flourish and with the exception of Greater London, no other county in England has seen such a proliferation of the breed, rejoicing under such names as Apple Barrel Press, Crypt Press, New Broom Press, Offcut Press, Silk Purse Press, Tie Press, and most intriguingly the Wind Tunnel Irregulars.

To complete this survey of the growth of the new movement of private presses in the 1950s and 1960s the Gogmagog Press of Morris Cox must be described. Cox was fifty-three when he founded Gogmagog in 1958, and he has since produced a series of most unusual and extremely interesting books. The press is unlike any other working in England today. It is not a hobby, but was set up to provide Cox with an effective means of realizing his own artistic and literary vision. He has an original talent and works very much within the tradition of William Blake, creating complete books at his press. Routledge had issued his first collection of poems, *Whirligig* in 1954, but they felt that his work would never be likely to sell in sufficient numbers to justify their publishing anything further. He overcame rejection by starting work on a 200 line poem, *Yule Gammon* (1957), printing it on a home made block-printing press using ten point Plantin type, and embellishing it with a handcoloured linocut frontispiece. Twenty copies were produced, but only a few had been sold before he decided the standard of production was too low and withdrew the edition.

Starting again in 1958 he issued his first book bearing the

Gogmagog imprint. *The slumbering virgin* was a blank-verse version of the very old story of the sleeping princess. It was well reviewed and represented a genuine advance in technique. Cox was now clear about his aims to publish original texts that were fully complemented by his own illustrations. His views on how this ought to be achieved give some indication of his unorthodoxy and self-reliance:

> No serious work should be attempted that can be done as well or better by the average commercial printer.
> Anything that will take ink and permit its transference to paper is a legitimate working material and constitutes printing.

He insisted that he should carry out all tasks by himself, no matter how small this made the resulting edition. He was no typographical purist and would accept an ugly typeface that fitted the mood of his work rather than compromise his intention. Many of his books left him feeling dissatisfied and some were never issued at all. *The Curtain* (1960) did come closer to his ideal, but he is restless and always seeking new ways of creating illustrations that will be better suited to his poems. His methods have developed to the point where he employs a combination of direct and offset printing, with hand-inking in several colours on blocks that he has built up from cardboard, lace, wire netting, dried leaves, and almost anything else he can think of to furnish his prints with the more than two-dimensional, tactile quality he is seeking. Today the limited editions of his books are distributed by Bertram Rota and he still produces them entirely by his own labour. Morris Cox is one of the best examples of that very tough and resiliant strain of private printer, the artist-poet, who, beginning with William Blake, have shown a remarkable resistance to the pressures of specialisation in modern society.

Chapter four

POETRY AND THE PRIVATE PRESS

Publishing new poetry by unknown poets seems to be full of uncertainty for the main commercial publishers as well as being something their accountants frown upon. Because of this it has been left to the private presses and small independent publishers to do their best for aspiring poets during most of the twentieth century. The private presses for their part have performed this important service to literature for more than fifty years, and this is all the more remarkable when it is remembered that most of them are only the spare-time occupations of their owners. Since the second world war poetry has become the largest single category of material to be published by private presses. Of the forty-five English presses included by Rae and Handley-Taylor in the *Book of the private press*, twelve printed poetry as their main activity and several others had published some poetry along with other things. Nearly all well-known contemporary poets such as Philip Larkin, Thom Gunn, Charles Tomlinson, Ted Hughes and Seamus Heaney have had their early work issued by private presses, and some continue to allow their poems to appear through these presses once they are established. This happens because poetry lends itself to publication in pamphlets and the small modern private presses are themselves very much suited to the production of literature in this format.

Philip Larkin's first book *The North Ship* (1945) appeared under the imprint of Reginald Caton's Fortune Press. Caton had been publishing poetry in Hessle, not far from Hull, since 1924. Ten years later Larkin had another collection of poems *The Less Deceived* published by the Marvell Press of George Hartley in Hull. Hartley also issued *The Minute Longer* by John Holloway and *Home Truths* by Anthony Thwaite. Erica Marx's Hand and Flower Press produced a series of monthly poetry pamphlets, beginning in 1951. Number one was Charles Causley's *Farewell Aggie Weston*, and among the many others were *Relations and Contraries* by Charles Tomlinson and Thomas Blackburn's *The Outer Darkness*.

In St Ives in 1951 Guido Morris produced a prospectus for the 'Crescendo Poetry Series', and the following extracts give some indication of the approach to poetry publishing adopted by the Latin Press which is also typical of the private press movement generally.

> The Publisher hopes to present unknown as well as established authors, all are invited to submit work . . . All expenses of publication, including mailing, will be borne solely by the Publisher, no Author will be asked to contribute anything, save his good will towards the series . . .
> The publisher undertakes to pay the Author a Royalty . . . on all copies sold.

There were eight titles published in the series before the Latin Press closed in 1953. Each title was issued in an edition of about 600 copies in paper covers, and sold for 2s 6d. Included was a translation of *Aphrodite's garland* by John Heath-Stubbs and collections of poems by Bernard Bergonzi, George Trakl and Guido Morris himself.

Oscar Mellor started the Fantasy Press to earn some much needed cash to enable him to continue painting. His first press was a small hand operated Adana with an inside chase measurement of 7 x 5 inches. Finding this inadequate he purchased an Adana T/P 48 treadle platen machine, adding another treadle press later, a Pershke Vicobold Crown Folio platen. The jobbing work was done mainly for Oxford University clubs and societies and consisted of theatre programmes, playbills, club membership cards and small magazines. From this he learned that to print well he should concentrate on working with a single typeface. Reflecting on his own experience he wrote:

> I would advise others starting upon the craft to select a main body fount, in, say, two point sizes, with italic to match; and to augment systematically with card founts in display sizes of the same face.

When he came to publish his poetry pamphlets he had settled on Times New Roman, which had been designed by Stanley Morison. Through his jobbing work Mellor had come to know members of the Oxford University Poetry Society, and gradually the idea developed of producing a series of small collections of poems by members of the society.

The Fantasy Poets series was launched in 1952, and the first one was an undated pamphlet containing seven poems by Elizabeth Jennings. Each pamphlet—and thirty-five were issued between 1952 and 1957—consisted of eight pages with six containing verse and the two remaining pages serving as the front and back covers. Editions ranged from 150 to 300 copies and at first sold for 9d with the price later increased to 1s. Oscar Mellor edited the pamphlets jointly with a series of partners, among whom were Michael Shanks, George MacBeth, and Bernard Bergonzi. Initially the poets included were only those from Oxford University. Later Cambridge poets were added and finally the series was opened to all poets whether members of a university or not. Other poets who had early collections published in the Fantasy series were Adrian Mitchell, Kingsley Amis, Philip Larkin, Thom Gunn and Donald Davie. A certain similarity of tone shared by some of the poets in the series detectable by readers of the relevant pamphlets led to some critics identifying a 'movement'. Robert Conquest voiced this in *New Lines* as 'a refusal to abandon a rational structure and comprehensible language, even when the verse is most highly charged with sensuous or emotional intent'. While these poets were a minority, it is nevertheless interesting to examine a checklist of books from the press to discover how many have stood the test of time and are still writing well.

Jack Hobbs and John Rolph were representatives travelling the London bookshops for established publishers when they decided to found the Scorpion Press in 1958. At that time, as John Rolph recalls, 'very few publishers had any poetry on their lists . . .'. They commissioned a commercial printer to produce the books for them while they found suitable poets. Rolph gives an amusing account of the way Bernard Kops was teased into writing poetry prior to the appearance of his *Poems and songs*, the first book from Scorpion Press:

> Bernard and I had been having a riotous time giving each other a first line every day—any mad phrase would do—from which we had each had to write a poem to be presented to the other the day following.

Following this, Christopher Logue's *The man who told his love*, an excellent adaptation from the work of Pablo Neruda, was published in December 1958. Robert Nye, a very young poet at the time, had a collection of poems *Juvenilia 1* (1961) issued by the press and he has continued writing since, establishing a considerable reputation as a poet and novelist. Several dozen books were issued by the press, and because the owners were well placed to distribute their output through the major London bookshops they all sold well, demonstrating once again that the market for poetry is there to be tapped, although largely ignored by the major publishers.

Concrete poetry is a series of objects depending upon the visual emphasis of a partly abstract typography to create a metaphor for the viewer of the poem. An international movement for the promotion of such objects began to influence English poets in the late 1950s. Many poems of this kind were issued on posters and cards, and a private press prominent in the genre was Ian Hamilton Finlay's Wild Hawthorn Press, which was established in 1961. His standing poems were printed on card and intended to be kept on display in the home in much the same way as greetings cards. Finlay's own poem *Earthship* (1965) was an attractively boxed variable construction with the words silkscreened on tensioned card. Wild Hawthorn published more than two dozen booklets during the 1960s and all of them were made to the same high standard. Among the poets associated with concrete poetry in this period, Finlay came to be regarded as the finest craftsman and most sensitive interpreter of the medium.

Poetry publishing was changing very rapidly in the 1960s and many new influences were emerging. Chief among these was the literature of the underground protest movements, and many younger writers and poets were seeking alternative ways of having their work published. One of the traditions they rejected was the letterpress printing of the private presses. This was replaced by duplicated typescripts, and poetry in this format was distributed and sold through a network of 'underground' shops. The poetry also rejected a good many of the usual grammatical and syntactical devices, but it generated a lot of interest and was obviously of value to the people who bought the typescripts. Edward Lucie-Smith, approving the work produced by these 'little presses', commented on their erecting 'a small untidy cairn raised to the spirit of human cussedness'.

The Association of Little Presses was founded in 1966 to bring together publishers and printers who were interested in printing a variety of texts in both prose and poetry. It is a loose association of presses and apart from holding exhibitions, like those at the American Embassy in 1968 and the National Book League in 1970, its activities have been directed towards the production of a catalogue. The first edition of the *Catalogue of little press books in print* was published in 1970. Several more have appeared since, and the recent issues have been produced on A4 sheets in duplicated typescript with the intention of issuing additional sheets to update the main work as the need arises. The current bibliography of the poetry from these presses has been recorded in *Poetry Information* for the last ten years. This review periodical has been issued twice each year by Peter Hodgkiss from his home in south-west London. It has been a remarkable achievement for one man, but he announced in number nineteen that only two further numbers were to appear after which it would cease publication. At the moment there are no plans for anything similar to take its place.

The little presses are intent on pursuing their own way and there is very little acknowledged connection between their work and that of the private presses, although few private printers would disagree with the sentiment of Stefan Themerson, owner of the Gaberbocchus Press, in his introduction to the fourth edition of the *Catalogue of little press books in print*:

> I can well imagine a perfectly healthy society in which nobody reads poetry. I cannot imagine a healthy society in which nobody writes poetry.

Roderick Cave, in *The Private Press*, writes briefly on the little presses and their similarity to modern private presses, concluding: 'It is a pity that there is this distance between these two groups of amateurs, for each has something of value to offer the other . . . '. These two groups inhabit different worlds, and although they would probably agree on many things related to the essential task of providing the means by which poetry can be published, they continue to follow divergent paths towards this goal.

Several of the private presses from among the many publishing poetry in the late 1960s are worthy of attention. Juliet Standing's Daedalus Press published *Twelve Poems* (1968) by R H Mottram with a dedicatory poem by Edmund Blunden and illustrations by Rigby Graham. Juliet Standing, apart from producing her own books, began printing for the Enitharmon Press of Alan Clodd. Among these books were *Communications* (1967) by Anna Madge Hopewell, with an engraving by Juliet Standing, and *Five dreams and other poems* by Kathleen Raine, with an engraving by Juliet Standing, in an edition of 450 copies including 75 specially bound by Trevor Hickman. The Sceptre Press was set up by Martin Booth out of the proceeds of his first BBC broadcast and was then subsidized by his literary earnings. Since 1970 the press has issued more than 160 titles usually in editions of no more than 150 copies. A poet himself, Martin Booth has published the work of both well known and unknown poets. Among the established poets have been Dannie Abse, Seamus Heaney and Sylvia Plath. Most titles go out of print very quickly and the unsigned copies retail at 45p to 90p.

Another poet, Boyd Lichfield, started Transican Books in Leicester, before moving to a stone cottage on the edge of the Charnwood Forest in Leicestershire. He used an Adana hand-quarto press to print his own poetry, and produced *The dissolving cuckoo* (1970) in an edition of 120 copies, on a purple grey mould-made paper with a red wraparound endpaper and a golden-yellow card cover, which quickly went out of print. Brian Patten's *Walking Out* was printed and published by Lichfield in an edition of 100 copies and case bound in black leather and offered for sale at seven guineas. This was quickly bought up by London booksellers. Even in private printing circles this press seems to have been a particularly doubtful undertaking, as Rigby Graham commented:

> Transican makes few or no concessions to anything. It is, as a press, wayward and unbusinesslike and rarely answers letters, and its productions are ethereal and odd.

One Leicestershire press which has made a success of publishing poetry is the New Broom Private Press of Toni Savage. Previously he had been a lyric tenor at Teatro al Fenice in Venice, but poor health obliged him to relinquish his career and he had turned to private printing, seeking an outlet for his creative energy. Helping with the Orpheus Press had been his introduction to printing and he was a partner in Pandora. After assisting with presswork at the Black Knight Press, Savage began working with his own press, printing two books and a pamphlet under the New Broom imprint, and since 1968 the press has been issuing pamphlets and broadsheets continuously.

In 1968 he produced *Cicadas* for Count Potocki of Montalk, and two years later in 1970 issued the same author's *Lammas Day*. One of the most satisfactory of the earlier booklets was

Lapus Calami by Boyd Lichfield with drawings by Franco Colavecchia. In 1969 he published a short poem, *Children of Aberfan*, by Spike Milligan, about the disaster in the Welsh village. Poetry has come to predominate in the output of the New Broom Private Press. Contemporary verse has been published for Jake Thackray, Colin Scot and Don Partridge. Toni Savage produced a substantial book of poems and song lyrics *Canticle Collection* (1971) by Rex Brisland, following this with two further books by the same poet— *Tryptych* and *Fairy Story*.

Since 1971 the press has become widely known for its series of broadsheets. The Phoenix Broadsheets, named after La Fenice Theatre in Venice, are well designed and carefully printed, and many have been distributed without charge to the Phoenix theatre audiences in Leicester. Toni Savage has built up his own collection of street literature, broadsheets and theatre bills. The broadsheets from New Broom were an extension of his interest in folk songs and the theatre. Each broadsheet in the series contains a poem or a short piece of prose and an illustration, many of which have been drawn by Rigby Graham. The first one included a poem *For Brian Patten* by Boyd Lichfield, and was illustrated by Duine Campbell. Others have contained the poems of Bernard Bresslaw, Spike Milligan, Jake Thackray, Brian Patten, John Cotton, Karla Hammond and Count Potocki of Montalk. *Phoenix Broadsheet One Hundred* included a verse by Jack Woolgar celebrating Toni Savage's continuing success which ended with the lines:

> he's now achieved his century
> and's still proliferating

A fitting sentiment for a private printer who has brought a great deal of ingenuity and imagination to the production of his press.

GRIND THE MILL

She's eaten three husbands into the ground
  (grind the mill round, grind)
All of them millers, strong and sound-
until she drove them out of their minds.

  (Grind round the barley, boys,
    grind into the ground)

She is as mad as a shuttlecock tossed,
lost in the mill-race and never found-
for she's eaten three husbands into the ground
now she hasn't two teeth to gnaw her toast.

(So its
  grind round the barley, boys,
    grind into the ground).

Cornish Aerie, poems by Richard Gilbertson. Printed by Toni Savage, New Broom Private Press. Opening containing poem 'Grind the Mill' and illustration by Rigby Graham.

Two private presses which publish poetry that have not been included here are Alan Tarling's Poet & Printer and Peter Scupham's Mandeville Press. They have very different ways of approaching their work and, together with Roy Lewis's Keepsake Press which also produces poetry, they are representative of the best in private press publishing practice. Their work will be described at length in Part two.

The private press is a suitable means of printing the work of a young poet who finds the world of the major publishers a bewildering and forbidding environment. Although a great deal of the poetry published by these presses is very bad, occasionally there appears a poet of talent and promise. By providing an outlet for poets who simply want the encouragement that comes from seeing their verse in print, the private press is serving their interests admirably, and the close personal relationship that the poet has with the printer allows him to concentrate upon his central task while someone who cares for poetry is looking after the boring and time-consuming details. Alan Brownjohn, writing in *The Author* of Spring 1968, emphasizes the usefulness of the private press:

> The private presses suffer from every conceivable disadvantage: fewer reviews for their books, uncertain distribution, no profitable lines to compensate for possible losses. But all these have in practice been counterbalanced time and again by the success of the volumes published . . . . Some of this success is also due to the loyalty and interest aroused by small experimental ventures . . . to people buying volumes from a . . . convinction that they are on to something exciting, worthwhile—and perhaps neglected.

The essence lies in the simplicity of the relationship created by the private printer. One man is bringing poet and reader together, cutting through the irrelevant complexity of the commercial world.

Chapter five

A LIVING TRADITION

In the second half of the twentieth century, private presses are having far less to do with improving the technical standards of book production than with extending and refining the coverage of the conventional publisher. They issue books on their own behalf which have marginal or even less commercial interest. Private printers are thriving in the interstices between the conglomerates. The commercial trade is being drawn towards the mass market where large sales and a streamlined product range are a recipe for success. Meanwhile the private press is helping to meet the needs of an increasing number of minority interests.

A writer in the *Times literary supplement*, April 26 1963, makes this comment on the purpose of the private press:

> Its existence constitutes a reproach or revolt against the public press, taking that word in its widest sense. Whether instituted to promulgate a revolutionary opinion, to publish avant-garde verse, to experiment with new methods of multiplying a pictorial image, . . . its origin lies in some real or imagined defect in the public press of the time.

For the private presses to be successful in combating these defects, public attention must be caught and then retained.

Since the second world war private printers have generally proved capable of drawing attention to themselves, and one of the best indications of continuing public interest in their work has been the number of successful exhibitions held in recent years. The King's Lynn Festival in 1967 was the occasion for one entitled 'The private press today', arranged by Juliet Standing. To place some limit on the amount of material to be included, only work produced in the previous ten years was included, and eventually publications from forty-three presses were assembled.

The majority of printers exhibiting were English, with representative presses from Italy, France, the USA and several other countries. Morris Cox of Gogmagog had a sequence of openings of all *Four Seasons* on display, together with blocks and openings from *Mummer's Fool* and *Triads*. Several books and poster poems from the Wild Hawthorn Press were displayed, and three copies of the periodical *Poor old tired horse* were included with them. Other presses showing their work were Rampant Lions, Keepsake, Fantasy and Ben Sands's Shoestring Press. Almost 1000 visitors viewed the exhibition between July 22 and 29, some returning several times to discuss what they had seen with the organizers. Juliet Standing, writing about the exhibition in *The Private Library*, criticized some presses for fighting battles that had been won in the early part of the twentieth century, remonstrating with them:

> Surely by now we can take the existence of good types, good papers, good taste, for granted and go on to use a press because there are things that need printing, are unlikely to be produced commercially . . . and are of value and interest to various sections of society

This cannot be repeated too often because the private press does have an important part to play in modern printing and publishing, and to do this effectively it must look to the future and not become absorbed by the past.

A comprehensive exhibition 'The Private Press' was mounted by the School of Librarianship at Loughborough

Technical College from May 6–11 1968. Roderick Cave was largely responsible for organizing the display, which covered the period from the mid-eighteenth century to the present day. It provided a useful complement to the King's Lynn exhibition of the previous summer. A number of exhibits had been lent by Cambridge and Oxford University Presses and some items came from the Birmingham Reference Library. Private collectors had been generous with their books, and other material had been drawn from the private press collection of the School of Librarianship itself. One eighteenth century book on show was a copy of Gray's *Odes* printed at the Strawberry Hill Press of Horace Walpole in 1757. Proof copies of *The Decameron* (1920) and *Don Quixote* (1927), issued by the Ashendene Press, were to be seen together with a selection of woodcuts used by the press.

Besides books there were blocks, specimen founts of type, punches and matrices displayed. A section of the exhibition was devoted to the Leicestershire presses and among those represented were the Brewhouse, Orpheus, Cog and Plough along with several others. An old Albion press in working order was manned by two keen students ready to help any visitors adventurous enough to try their hands at pulling a keepsake of the exhibition. Those who did try went away with their still wet sheet feeling very pleased with themselves. Roderick Cave wrote the text for *The Private Press: handbook to an exhibition*, a small handsome volume providing an illustrated history of the private press from its beginnings to the latest happenings in Leicestershire. It was printed in Bembo type in an edition of 600 copies by Thomas Rae at the Grian-aig Press, and 150 copies were bound by Trevor Hickman.

Paul Peter Piech, who runs the Taurus Press of Willow Dene, was the driving force behind two exhibitions in the Central Library, Watford. The first was held in 1969 when only five printers, members of the London Chappel, participated; and the second, much larger one, in 1970 featured presses from Leicester and London. Both exhibitions were planned to illustrate the range of contemporary private printing. From the first only Kenneth Hardacre's booklet *The private press in Hertfordshire*, containing his opening address, survives, and in this speech he examined the nature of the private press: 'Private press printing is personal printing, and, quoting Eric Gill's definition: 'A private press prints solely what it chooses to print', continued with this observation on the exhibits:

> Here around you are examples of the freedom of the press in the most real and literal sense, a positive and not a negative freedom, a creative and not merely a concessional freedom.

Freedom to print what one chooses is of fundamental importance to the private printer; conversely the continued existence of the private press helps in some small way to guarantee that freedom.

The work of seventeen presses was on display at the second Watford exhibition: ten of these came from London and seven from Leicestershire. Among those from Leicestershire were the Brewhouse, Cog and Plough presses. London provided classical typography from the Laverlock Press of Iain Bain with an opening of his edition of John Bell's *Albium de Novo Castro 1807-1864*. Bain, an expert on Thomas Bewick, also exhibited prints taken from the original blocks engraved by Thomas Bewick and his apprentices. Paul Peter Piech contributed several imposing linocuts, while Ben Sands had sent his humorous *A is an apple pie*. There were no catalogues produced for either exhibition and information regarding books and other exhibits must be gleaned from the few contemporary accounts of writers like Rigby Graham and Kenneth Hardacre.

A handsome quarto catalogue describing the contributions from 183 private presses was printed at the Foulis Archive Press, in an edition of 400 copies, to mark the occasion of an impressive exhibition 'The Page Right Printed' held in Glasgow from May 1-12 1973 in Charles Rennie Macintosh's Glasgow School of Art. The exhibits illustrated the work of private presses from William Morris to the present day. The Golden Cockerel Press was represented by *Twelfth Night, the True History of Lucian* with engravings by Robert Gibbings, and Jack Lindsay's *Storm at Sea* with engravings by John Farleigh. There were also specimen pages from *Paradise Lost* and the *Four Gospels*. The Poet & Printer of Alan Tarling displayed Alan Dixon's *Upright position* and Peter Redgrove's *Three pieces for voices*, and there was a collection of Phoenix Broadsheets from Toni Savage. The exhibition was well planned and considerable thought was given to the layout of individual exhibits. The high standard of private press work throughout the period was very much in evidence.

Two further exhibitions, from among the many that have been held, should be mentioned. In November 1973 an exhibition of books from Trevor Hickman's Brewhouse Press was held in the Library at Austin Peay State University, Clarksville, Tennessee, bringing international recognition to one of Britain's most interesting presses. Earlier Roderick Cave had written about work from the press being

> different from that of any other art work in England today: sumptuous binding enclosing important and interesting text admirably illustrated and with an unusual disregard for typographical niceties.

Rudas

In the dark Turkish bath-house,
Under the flattened medieval dome
Where sounds and voices fall
And bounce along the lappled surface
Of the central circular bath
And its four corner spandrel pools
Fed by spouting springs,
Hot, tepid, warm, and cool;
Beneath these water levels
Dim algae float, move, drift,
Subaqueous shapes, distorted limbs,
With linen ephods trailing in sluggish currents,
Damp drapery hiding, revealing, tufts of pubic hair
That wave their warning signals, and wreathe
Shy pendent penes, wrinkled scrota,
Scarce stirring in their private lairs,
Pale weeds,
Timeless in long suspense –
Suddenly through a chink of coloured glass
Inset in the dome a spear of sunlight
Strikes down across the steamy gloom
And stabs an unseen body
Sitting on an unseen step,
Leaving a minute radiant patch
On chance shoulder or chance thigh for a brief moment
As the sun's minute finger passes by.

The Gentle Pagan

1

Flushed with the heat of the hall,
The two of us left the island dance
With the band still thumping out its beat.

After walking down to the midnight beach,
We cast off in your fishing boat.
Each of us found the crossing to Tresco
Cool and deliciously quiet.

At Old Grimsby the tide was dead low,
And we couldn't make the jetty;
So I bent down to undo my laces
And take off my dancing shoes
In order to wade ashore.

But before I was ready, you'd stepped overboard
And lifted me up in your arms
As if I had been of little weight;
And as you carried me steadily
Above the shifting fluorescent shoals,
I was startled after so long a gap
To feel myself a child again.

2

Years later,
Sailing between these islands towards Crow Sound,
Your eyes fixed on familiar rocks and marks,
Hand on tiller, suddenly you released your grip
And slipped away from us across the Bar –
A gentle Pagan seeking Lyonesse.

New Beginnings, poems by Eric Walter White. Printed by Alan Tarling, Poet and Printer. Opening p28 & p29 containing 'Rudas' and 'The Gentle Pagan'.

The variety of work from the press stems from Hickman's avowal that 'the pleasure comes from designing afresh and tackling new problems each time'. A representative collection of Brewhouse books was displayed alongside an almost complete set of Brewhouse Broadsheets.

To celebrate William Caxton's introduction of printing to Britain in 1476 an 'Exhibition of books and printed ephemera from twenty-eight contemporary private presses' was opened by Douglas Cleverdon at the Swiss Cottage library on December 3 1976. An attractive catalogue reveals that among the presses involved were Cuckoo Hill, Gogmagog, Kit-Cat, Rampant Lions, Taurus, Whittington and World's End, representing a cross-section of the best of today's private printers.

While exhibitions enable private printers to maintain and extend their contacts with the general public, they also serve the secondary purpose of keeping them in touch with one another. Periodicals on the other hand are primarily directed towards other printers or serious book collectors, but are able on occasion to generate interest among ordinary readers. A number of new journals have been appearing since the mid-1960s either entirely devoted to private printing or prepared to grant some space to the subject. One or two of them have managed to survive beyond their initial period of enthusiasm, but others have lasted only for a year or two before being closed. The monthly *Small Printer* was first published in 1965 and continues today as the official journal of the British Printing Society. Apart from recording the social activities and business of the society it consists mainly of practical articles for the jobbing printers who make up the majority of the membership. These are useful to the private printer and in any case joining the society brings the opportunity to purchase printing supplies at a discount. Occasionally the editor of *Small Printer* accepts an article from a private printer. Alan Tarling has had several published, as has Kenneth Hardacre, who has enjoyed the added distinction of being elected president of the society.

Rigby Graham's periodical *Private Printer & Private Press* (1968) lasted for one issue, despite the editor's modest intention of only producing 100 copies of each issue. *The Printing Art*, published quarterly by James Moran during 1973 and 1974, was very similar in intention and format to *The Black Art*, which he produced during the 1960s, although it was produced lithographically and not by letterpress. A book-collector's journal, *Antiquarian Book Monthly Review*, which started in February 1974 carries an occasional article on some aspect of private press activity and these are usually very good.

More interesting than most of the others, and hopefully here to stay, is *Albion* which was started in 1977 and is published three times a year by Roger Burford Mason at the Dodman Press, Hitchin. This is an attractive magazine produced on A4 paper in duplicated typescript with the sheets stapled together inside covers of varying colours. It is totally dedicated to furthering the cause of private printing and regular features include descriptions of individual presses and their publications, interviews with printers and poets, and short reviews of recent books from the presses. The annual subscription of only £1.50 including postage makes *Albion* very good value indeed.

Since 1945 there have been more than 600 active private presses in England. Most have survived for only a short time, and those enjoying a continuous existence for more than a decade are exceptional. It is impossible to put an accurate figure on how many are working at present. The *Basilisk Catalogue* (1978) includes more than seventy, and the most recent issue of *Private Press Books*, forty-six. Allowing for some overlap between these lists, it would be reasonable to place the number of active private printers at around one hundred.

In these large numbers lies their strength. Julia Horsfall in 'Notes on the small presses in Britain', *British Book News*, September 1978, concludes with the following passage:

> When the small presses lose their diversity and the cussed determination to publish what they want, which is their glory and occasionally their ruin, they might as well cease to exist, for the job of mass publication of the books everybody reads is done better elsewhere.

There is no sign of any reduction in the diversity of private presses working in the late 1970s, as those described below serve to illustrate.

Paul Peter Piech came originally from Brooklyn, where he received his formal training as an artist. Living for the last thirty years in England, he has spent most of his working life in advertising. It was in 1959 that he established his press at his home in Bushey Heath. The Taurus Press has always had a social message and this reflects Piech's humanitarian views and opposition to all forms of violence. His early books seem to have been printed on almost any paper that came to hand, their typefaces were hardly ever suited to their texts but they retain their power to make one uncomfortable. The linocuts and woodcuts have great force and compassion. Kenneth Hardacre describes this succinctly: 'For Paul Piech expresses pity with his knife'. The cover of his first production, *War & Misery*, bears a woodcut of a manacled hand pressed against barbed wire. The foreword explains that the woodcuts in the book record 'the horrors, miseries and degradations of man's ignoble acts towards his fellow man'.

In the 1960s Piech produced a series of cards bearing

short quotations, for which the entire text had been cut by hand in lino. Soon after starting these he acquired a large proofing press and was able to apply this method in his book, William Blake's poem *London*. He is strongly influenced by events such as Watergate or Nixon's statement that if he picked up a telephone and gave the appropriate orders, 70 million people would die within twenty-five minutes. He hardly ever uses type in his posters and the text which he cuts by hand is given added urgency by the manner of cutting. He makes no preliminary design but creates the letter as he cuts. Recently he has begun to explore quieter forms, taking as his themes the shapes taken by natural growth.

In complete contrast, John and Rosalind Randle publish superbly illustrated books in limited editions at the Whittington Press. They started their press as a hobby in 1971 in the Cotswold village of Andoversford. After the success of their first books, Richard Kennedy's *A boy at the Hogarth Press* and J B Priestley's *Happy Dream*, they were able to turn it into a full-time small publishing house. All their books are printed by hand on one of their Victorian hand-presses or machined on a small Wharfdale. They also run three-day printing courses twice each year, covering basic typographical design, hand-setting and press work. Currently they are experimenting with hand-made paper using papyrus from the garden pond, but it is not yet a commercial proposition. The press issues four or five books each year with maximum editions of around 500 copies. One of their more interesting productions is William Nicholson's *An Alphabet*, a collection of thirty-eight wood engravings on single unbound sheets, cased in a cloth-covered drop-back box, together with a booklet about the engravings by Edward Craig.

Two other presses catering for similar tastes are the Rainbow Press of Olwen Hughes, which she started in 1971 to print limited editions of the poems of both her brother Ted Hughes and Sylvia Plath, later adding Thom Gunn, Ruth Fainlight and Seamus Heaney, and the Tern Press of Nicholas and Mary Parry founded in 1975 which produces finely printed bilingual editions of Celtic and Anglo-Saxon texts.

The World's End Press of Ann Brunskill is dedicated to the production of fine books which provide vehicles for her own illustrations. Her work has more in common with the French 'livre d'artiste' than with anything in the English private press tradition. In the earliest book from the press, *Aphrodite: a mythical journey in eight episodes* (1970), the 36pt Baskerville italic balances the facing illustrations perfectly. The etchings are deeply bitten on steel and printed in two closely related tones with a contrasting third colour. Ann Brunskill is an original artist of great technical skill with a lively imagination. The most recent of her books, *Thomas Traherne: Poems and Centuries* (1978) has text printed in 24pt Baskerville roman with eight mixed media prints and a colour etched title page by the artist and shows definite development in her technique. It is so far the most complex experimental work to come from the press.

Fiction publishing has not been widespread among private presses in the past, but it will probably be undertaken more frequently in future. The commercial presses are finding that novels and short stories are less profitable than they used to be. Already little presses like Aloes Books and Lunatic Fringe Publications are able to produce such work, using typewriters and offset-litho machines. They can produce a thousand copies of a book of approximately 150 pages for about £500 adding £200 for distribution costs, and selling copies for just under £1 to cover costs of materials and overheads. Geoffrey Wakeman at the Plough Press, which will be described in Part two, makes this level of investment in the specialist books he publishes and finds it profitable to do so.

The opportunities are there, and already Roy Lewis at the

Keepsake Press has issued a small volume of Roy Fuller's previously unpublished short stories in an edition of 275 copies. The private printers will probably be able to publish short stories and novellas quite successfully, particularly if they are prepared to become book designers, using their hand-presses to produce camera-ready copy, and leaving actual printing to the instant print-shops who produce very good work using the techniques of offset-lithography and thermographic copying. It is possible that the problems of producing satisfactory prose texts may bring the private printers and little press printers closer together. Julia Horsfall thinks the divisions are no longer relevant:

> ... the phenomenon of independent book and pamphlet production in Britain now transcends the usual distinctions of letter press versus litho, hand-printing versus commercial printing, and it should be seen as a whole.

There will be many private printers and little press printers opposed to such changes, but a minority will adapt these techniques to their own work, extending the scope of private printing and adding to their chances of survival.

Part two

EIGHT CONTEMPORARY
PRIVATE PRESSES

PRELIMINARY NOTE

Part two is devoted to a small selection of contemporary private presses which together make up a representative cross-section of current practices and present the opportunity for a closer examination of the motives and aspirations of the printer-publishers themselves.

Charlene Garry at the Basilisk Press must be included because her bookshop has so quickly become an important focus for many private printers and collectors.

David Chambers too is an obvious choice. For, apart from running the Cuckoo Hill Press, he is a founder member of the Private Libraries Association and the Society of Private Printers, and in addition has been one of the editors of *Private Press Books* since its earliest years.

Kenneth Hardacre is a fine printer at the Kit-Cat Press who has never ceased to improve the standard of his work. No one else has achieved as much as he with the small Adana 8 x 5 inch press.

Roy Lewis at the Keepsake Press has been publishing poetry longer than any other private printer and while very much alive to the tradition of hand-printing, he is always ready to try something new that might usefully extend his skills.

Alan Tarling has built up a considerable reputation at the Poet & Printer as a sympathetic but shrewd printer-publisher of modern poetry.

Peter Scupham is a poet who runs the Mandeville Press for the benefit of other poets whose work might otherwise not be printed.

Geoffrey Wakeman at the Plough Press publishes scholarly works on out-of-the-way typographical subjects, and enjoys a small but thriving export trade in his books.

Ben Sands, originally a commercial artist and now a book designer, has been able to express himself in a skilful and vivacious manner in his beautifully executed linocuts. Books from the Shoestring Press are quickly taken up by collectors.

The dates of foundation of these eight presses parallel the development of private printing during the last thirty years. Four were started in the period of the first flowering of the new movement in the 1950s, two in the 1960s and two in the 1970s. Of the three presses issuing poetry, one was started in each of the three decades under review in this study. The most recent confirmation of the strength of public interest in private press books came with the opening of the Basilisk Press Bookshop in 1977.

The accounts given below are arranged in chronological sequence according to the foundation dates of the presses, and they are supplemented by selective checklists of their publications in the Appendix.

Chapter six

THE CUCKOO HILL PRESS

David Chambers, who is an underwriter at Lloyds, devotes his free time to interests in printing history, bibliography, collecting private press books and printing on his own hand-press. Since 1961 he has been one of the editors of *Private Press Books*. His bibliographical work and the assistance he gives John Cotton, editor of *The Private Library*, significantly reduce the time he has for printing. He works carefully, planning everything in detail, even the most ephemeral French-fold.

Most things printed at the Cuckoo Hill Press in Pinner are securely based on relevant historical sources. To locate what he needs he begins by leafing through Stanley Morison's *Four centuries of fine printing*, going when inspiration is lacking to his own excellent library. Having found what he is looking for he sets out to re-create his discovery. Printing on his Demy Folio Albion (an Alexandra press made by Esson in 1884) is meticulously executed. The press is always accurately adjusted, with a new tympan for each production, and he employs type-high bearers to ensure a clean and well balanced impression. Typesetting extensive texts or printing long runs of anything bores him, and he prefers producing limited edtions of notes on the history of printing, or the careful proofing of wood engravings. He makes a point of using the best materials available. Romanée, Bembo and Fournier are his principal typefaces, and occasionally he will resort to machine typesetting to achieve a particular effect. Ink for the hand-roller must be stiff and the hand-made paper is always carefully dampened before printing. When he has particularly delicate work to do he likes to use Japanese papers. Binding is difficult, good bookbinders are rare and this aspect of the work he produces seems to give him least satisfaction. He is a perfectionist to the extent that he would prefer to have people print on only one side of a sheet of vellum because of the difference in the quality of the respective surfaces.

Irritation with mass-produced Christmas cards caused him to begin making designs for printing presses. Later he visited the printing shops on City Road, purchased an old office copying press for £2, and obtained some worn type, furniture, leads, chases and other odds and ends. Modifying the press took time but eventually he succeeded, and, as his description of the mechanism he constructed reveals, it was of unusual design:

> Hinged boards serve as a treadle, and, joined to a wire running over a pulley, draw the carriage (a hinged wooden frame for the type and paper) under the press; three springs, at the end of another wire running over another pulley, draw the carriage out again when the press is opened.

Printing began at the Cuckoo Hill Press in 1950 and for six years David and his father produced a stream of jobbing work. They printed around two hundred different posters, dance tickets, handbills, letter heads etc. The first booklet from the press was *Fireflies* (Christmas 1955) produced in a small edition of fifteen copies, containing seven small white-line engravings of sailing dinghies. Buying boxwood blocks for his engravings from 'Mr Lawrence's shop in Bleeding Heart Yard' also brought him into contact with European and Japanese hand-made papers. He became fascinated with these and started to collect them. The outcome of this was *Some Decorative Japanese Papers* (1960), a zig-zag folder produced for the Society of Private Printers and printed on his recently acquired Demy Folio Albion. *The Office Press*, an account of the construction of his home-made press, was published in 1961.

Elizabeth II Numismata (1964) contained thirteen prints made from coins of the realm, demonstrating David Chambers's increasingly skilful use of his press. The impressions are absolutely clear, and in order to achieve this from such low relief the inking had to be done very carefully to avoid any risk of printing the background of the image.

Slowly the range of his printing extended, and when together with Iain Bain he purchased fifty original woodblocks, engraved by Bewick and his school from Sotheby's, he was able to essay one of the most satisfying productions he has so far completed. *Engravings on wood* by Thomas Bewick and his pupils was finally completed in an edition of only sixteen copies in 1971. These were not sold but given to friends of the printer. Many of his productions have been issued in small editions in accordance with his view of private printing:

> I don't regard the press as a way of multiplying words so much as a means of creating something that may give pleasure to likeminded enthusiasts, and although I find perfection in printing well-nigh unattainable there is a lot of satisfaction to be had in the attempt.

Another feature of his printing is the length of time that may elapse before he brings something to completion. He was translating Pierres's *Description d'une Nouvelle Presse d'Imprimerie*, 1786, as long ago as 1963, and he has yet to start printing his English edition.

Chapter seven

THE SHOESTRING PRESS

Many private printers work slowly and their output is very small, but few are able to match the quality of the books that have come from the Shoestring Press, Whitstable, since 1952. Ben Sands is an artist who creates complete books in his own style. He would not claim to belong to any tradition, but rather sees himself practising the many skills he has learnt during his long career as a book designer. An apposite desscription of these skills is given by Joseph Moxon in *Mechanick exercises on the whole art of printing* (1683):

> . . . one who by his own judgement, from solid reasoning within himself, can either perform, or direct others to perform from the beginning to the end all the handyworks and physical operations relating to typographie.

Ben Sands is a very good typographer and the demands for his services from the commercial world are such that he is faced with the constant lure of freelance work, in addition to his normal job, and this distracts him from his avocation.

The Shoestring Press lives up to its name. All the equipment is as simple as it possibly can be. The printing press he has had longest is a Model Four hand-platen press to which is fitted a section from a table leg to improve leverage. The resulting impression bites deeply into the paper, almost crushing the type, and the crisp appearance matches that from any of the larger Albions. He frequently prints on dampened paper and selects typefaces which will blend well with his linocuts. The faces he uses—Bell Roman, Stephenson

Blake Modern No 20 and Goudy Kennerley—are merely the best he can find, because he is not at all satisfied with any that are currently available. For Ben Sands his printing and linocutting are 'a form of controlled drug taking', and he becomes deeply preoccupied with finding the correct typographical solution to the particular printing problem he has in hand.

He sees linocutting as a job for one man. From the initial design, through preliminary drawings and actual cutting, to the final proofing and printing he works carefully testing his ideas at every stage. Some books from the press have been illustrated with linocuts in black and white or in just a single colour, but for others he has developed a technique of graduated colour printing. To do this he stops the revolving inkplate on his press, and rolls several different coloured inks on it, causing the boundaries between the colours to merge, creating a subdued effect not unlike shot-silk. He then prints each sheet taking care to maintain the colour balance. The first book in which he used this technique was *The Walrus and the Carpenter* (1958).

He seems constantly to question the value of private printing, and he asks himself, 'how much room in life for it' should there be? Consequently it takes several years for him to produce a book, and the latest one to be published, *A dissertation upon roast pig* by Charles Lamb, was completed in 1975. At present he is planning another, an illustrated edition of Voltaire's tale *Micromegas*. He has produced a draft layout with the complete text printed in closely set Kennerley Bold with an unjustified right-hand margin. So far only one linocut has been completed, a double title page spread with lettering and illustration cut into one piece of lino. Unable for the moment to proceed, he feels that when eventually he does produce enough linocuts and is able to see the work as a whole, he will be on the way to making his

DICK AND SAL AT CANTERBURY FAIR

An early 19th Century Poem
in the Kentish Dialect
of the period

**HAND-PRINTED
ILLUSTRATED & PUBLISHED
BY BEN SANDS AT HIS
SHOESTRING PRESS
WHITSTABLE
1973**

Dick and Sal at Canterbury Fair, printed by Ben Sands, Shoestring Press.
Opening containing title page and illustration by Ben Sands.

best book so far. On the evidence of the title page and the trial settings of the text, it is not difficult to agree with him.

Chapter eight

THE KEEPSAKE PRESS

For Roy Lewis at The Keepsake Press in Richmond, Surrey, a private printer is what he is because of having taught himself to print by a process of trial and error. Typographers and professional printers printing in their spare time do not qualify. His policy as a small publisher of poetry is to publish only those things that have not yet appeared in print. There must also be a public, no matter how small, for the productions of the press, ready to pay 'good money' to buy the books. He is equally forthright about the role of the private printer:

> What he prints is exactly what the commercial publisher cannot, and that leaves him with a large, even growing, field for finding worthwhile manuscripts.

The Keepsake Press is not allowed to intrude too far into Roy Lewis's life. He is very clear about his determination to keep printing in its proper place in his order of priorities. His career as a journalist on *The Economist* and *The Times* has involved him in extensive travel and at least one long period of work overseas, which makes it seem all the more remarkable that he has been able to publish so many poetry pamphlets. His practical approach to the business of private printing and the amount of hard work he puts in at the press should not be allowed to obscure the fact that his aim is to enjoy the hobby and find relaxation from the cares of the world.

Since 1957 he has published more than one hundred pamphlets, most, but not quite all of them, containing the first printings of new poetry. In *The practice of parlour printing considered as a specific against insomnia and like disorders*

(1975) which he calls an 'apologia pro vita mea' he claims:

> I calculate that the Keepsake Press has printed and sold in all about 65,000 separate pages of poetry (exclusive of pages of illustrations or prelims) to the British and American public. It is not much, but it is a tributary to the great river.

Roy Lewis likes to combine poetry with illustrations in the pamphlets he publishes, and one of his more difficult problems is finding illustrators he can afford. The retail value of one of his editions is unlikely to exceed £300, and any reasonably well known artist who asks for a fee of around £100 is outside his budget. So he looks for students in local Colleges of Art whose work appeals to him, pays a smaller fee and enables the student to benefit through having some of his or her work published. He does all the jobs necessary to produce his pamphlets. He selects the text, designs, prints and binds the completed work, receiving some assistance from his wife with sewing the sections. He then wholesales or retails the finished product and does the bookkeeping, ensuring that costs of publication, excluding his own and his wife's time, are covered.

Acquiring a Columbian press—in time to be included in the *Book of the private press*—he began printing, using several full founts of type: Bell Roman, Times New Roman, Black Letter and a few titling and display founts of Albertus, Bodoni Bold, Gill Cursive and Latin Antique. He worked abroad for a while and had to sell the Columbian. When he returned he bought a Model Four platen press and began printing in a shed in his rose garden. From these new premises he issued Miss Austen's *The History of England* (1962) with seven linocuts by his daughter, Elizabeth Lewis. This was followed in the same year by *Poems in India* by Francis Watson.

Among other poets he has published have been Gavin Ewart, Edward Lowbury, Mervyn Peake, Peter Porter and previously unpublished work by James Elroy Flecker. The series of *Keepsake Poems* 'intended to be a single experience—the poet's ear and the artist's eye in one apprehension' began in 1972. Thirty-nine have appeared to date, each one containing a single poem accompanied by a single illustration. If any criticism can be levelled at them it is that the illustration sometimes overwhelms the poem and the centre-fold of the four page pamphlet appears unbalanced. Vernon Scannell, Christopher Logue and Wes Magee are among the poets who have appeared in the series. The illustrators have included John Piper, Paul Peter Piech and Rigby Graham.

Recently Roy Lewis has begun to think seriously about changing over to photo-setting and offset-litho, so that if he wanted to handle longer texts he could do so more comfortably. Although he enjoys setting type and printing by hand, he speculates:

> Who would now use hand composition, . . . in competition with the IBM typewriter?

After his experience of producing a twenty-six page book of short stories, *The Other Planet* by Roy Fuller in an edition of 275 copies (1979), he has become even more convinced of the value of the instant printshop. He would use his handpress to design books, preparing camera-ready copy and sub-contracting the printing to a competitive photo-offset printer.

Chapter nine

THE KIT-CAT PRESS

In the same way that Will Carter at the Rampant Lions Press sets the standard in printing for the entire modern private press movement in England, so does Kenneth Hardacre at the Kit-Cat Press, Kings Langley, set the standard for the miniature private press printer who produces only small books and pamphlets. There are interesting parallels between the paths followed by the two men, although they did not meet until some years after Kenneth Hardacre had begun printing. Like Carter, Hardacre was interested in calligraphy, and quite independently he came upon the typefaces of Herman Zapf, eventually deciding to use the Palatino and Optima types for his printing.

In the 1950s he had become concerned about the poor state of his hand-writing. He was convinced there was nothing he could do about this until he discovered a book about italic scripts. It gave no assistance with methods of letter formation, but did include illustrations of different italic styles, mostly reproduced from Renaissance manuscripts. He chose one he liked and started to copy it. However after a few months he looked at the book again and decided he liked a different one. This chopping and changing went on for some time until he finally made up his mind to consult the leading expert in the field. He sought the advice of Alfred Fairbank and was advised to buy the excellent Dryad writing cards, since when he has continued to practise the craft. One by-product of this affected his work as a teacher of English literature. His pupils noticed the change in his writing on the blackboard in class and asked to be taught to write in the same manner. This he did and found himself caught up in a dispute in the columns of the *Times literary supplement* with other teachers, who claimed that the proper place to teach handwriting was the art class. Kenneth Hardacre is still of the opinion that the English class is a more appropriate place.

Practising italic handwriting stimulated his curiosity about the ways in which the letters were formed, and this in turn led him to take up private printing. He is a self-concious craftsman and, in his own words,

> a professional man who finds satisfaction and self-expression in the craft aspect of his hobby, who prints because he enjoys printing, and prints what he pleases and when he pleases, having to meet neither deadline nor demand imposed upon him by someone else.

The first press he used was an Adana 8 x 5 inch hand-platen. He makes it clear that his primary interest lies in the activity of printing itself, and in consequence the papers he prints on and the typefaces he prints with are of fundamental importance to him. He makes extensive use of Basingwerk parchment and Mellotex high white paper for the text pages of his pamphlets; for the covers he uses Tumba Ingres cover paper and Strathmore Artlaid. He is fully convinced of the need to have 'good stock' to print on, otherwise the work would be ruined. Bembo was the first typeface he printed with and he still uses it occasionally, feeling that it is probably the most beautiful face ever designed. Unfortunately it cannot be had in founder's metal that is hard enough to satisfy his exacting requirements. Ultimately he did find something that came up to the standard he wanted. After having become fascinated by the Palatino and Optima types, he discovered that Arnold Cook of Hoddesdon were agents for the Stempel foundry where all Zapf's hot-metal types are cast, and for the last fifteen years

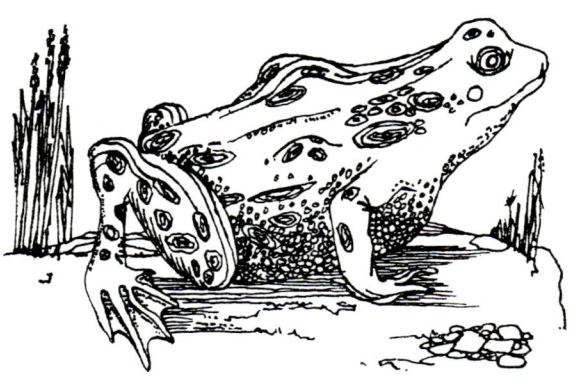

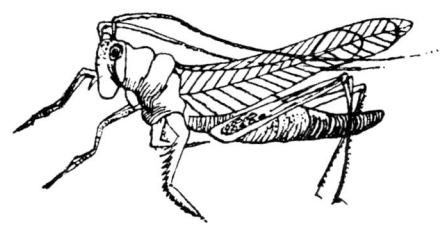

DAMON THE MOWER

Heark how the Mower *Damon* Sung,
With love of *Juliana* stung!
While ev'ry thing did seem to paint
The Scene more fit for his complaint.
Like her fair Eyes the day was fair;
But scorching like his am'rous Care.
Sharp like his Sythe his Sorrow was,
And wither'd like his Hopes the Grass.

Oh what unusual Heats are here,
Which thus our Sun-burn'd Meadows sear!
The Grass-hopper its pipe gives ore;
And hamstring'd Frogs can dance no more.
But in the brook the green Frog wades;
And Grass-hoppers seek out the shades.
Only the Snake, that kept within,
Now glitters in its second skin.

Damon the mower, four poems by Andrew Marvell. Printed by Kenneth Hardacre, Kit-Cat Press. Opening containing poem 'Damon the Mower' and illustrations of a frog and a grasshopper by Frederick Palmer.

he has continued to use these two faces with increasing skill.

When he began printing on the Adana he only produced things to give away to friends and other printers. People who liked what he did showed his work to their friends. Gradually demand for his printing began to grow, and he found he could sell his pamphlets to an increasing number of people. Each edition he prints now is of approximately 200 copies, which though not large, does meet the demands of a very keen group of collectors. Recently he has acquired a Vicobold treadle-platen press that has an electric motor attached to it, and it is probable that the number of titles he publishes and the sizes of the editions will be increased, to match the still growing demand. Nothing however will persuade him to compromise the very high standard of craftsmanship he has achieved.

Pamphlets from the Kit-Cat Press are scrupulously executed. The impression of type is always very black and crisp, with each opening perfectly balanced. He regularly uses coloured end-papers and covers in different shades, which, while blending together, contrast elegantly with the text pages. The whole booklet is smartly trimmed and carefully sewn, making something which is pleasing to read and satisfying to handle. In the series of pamphlets containing poems by Andrew Marvell—*Damon the Mower* (1975), *The Garden* (1976) and *To his coy mistress and other poems* (1978)—he has successfully introduced illustrations on the covers and into the texts, adding yet another attractive feature to an already impressive output. In future it will be by such carefully considered stages that Kenneth Hardacre will enhance his books.

Chapter ten

POET & PRINTER

The name of Alan Tarling's press, the Poet & Printer, at Hatch End, sets out his order of priorities. He is much more concerned with the poetry between the covers of his pamphlets than with their printing and binding. Poetry is very important to him—'Poetry is holy, one poem read is worth a hundred fondled'.

He pays his poets ten per cent of the retail price and guarantees to carry on paying them at this level no matter how many copies he might sell. Profit is not something that worries him, but he covers the costs of the press and the printing. Costing is done for each pamphlet in much the same way that a commercial publisher would do it. The difference is that Alan Tarling places payment to the poet at the top of the list. He adopts as professional an approach to being a printer-publisher as he can. In the costing of each production a further ten per cent is included to pay a free-lance publishers' representative, should one ever be needed, to wholesale his pamphlets to booksellers. One day he expects to publish the first poems of another Ted Hughes, and he does not intend to relinquish his success to any commercial publisher. In hoping for this he regards himself as a 'betting man', devoting his time and labour to bringing the best poetry he can find to his customers.

Estimating serious poetry readership in England at around 5000 people, he thinks that ideally he ought to be able to sell 1500 copies of every pamphlet he prints. If he then produced one pamphlet each month, he would be able to become a full-time publisher, and make a satisfactory living out of it. As things are, working on a part-time basis, he still prints and sells between four and five hundred copies of each title, and estimates that it takes approximately eighteen months to clear all the copies printed. The hard core of his customers, whom he refers to as 'loyalists', buy everything he publishes. These are the best sort; he gets to know them quite well, and this helps in maintaining the personal bond between his poets and their readers. He makes a point of replying to all enquiries and supplying all orders, by return of post. Also each order is met with fresh copies because he keeps his stock in sheets and only binds to order.

Manuscripts are regularly sent to him, and he finds himself giving advice to many young poets about what they should read and how they ought to set about improving their work. The advice is always the same: he refers them to the early poems of Ted Hughes and suggests they discover why these poems are so good. In doing this he makes no claims to any extensive knowledge of literature, but by applying what he terms 'basic literary standards' he has come to the conclusion that there is no better place for the aspiring poet to begin. Also he feels he has an advantage in not being a poet himself, as this provides him with a detached vantage point from which he can judge the work he receives and then offer what help he can. Alan Tarling likes to publish poetry that communicates itself to the reader in terms of rhythm, echoes, images, insight, an intuitive feeling of completeness, and above all in terms of telling a good story. He has no sympathy for the sort of poetry he refers to as 'academic crossword puzzles', because he says he wants to issue poems that will sell in his small editions; he has no intention of publishing for posterity.

When he started printing he was an 'absolute beginner'. He bought a small Adana 8 x 5 inch press, joined the British Printing Society, and acquired full founts of 12pt Poliphilus, 12pt Blado Italic and titling founts in 14pt and 24pt Bembo. At this time he recalls he had: 'too much enthusiasm for too little skill'.

The first pamphlet he printed was for the editor of a duplicated poetry magazine which he found in a bookshop in Charing Cross Road. Alan Tarling wrote to the magazine, offering to produce an anthology of their best work in 500 copies of twenty-four pages each; the editor wanted 750 copies of thirty-two pages each. They struck a bargain and the career of a new printer was launched. After taking nearly three difficult months to do the job he succeeded in completing it just one day inside his deadline. He paused and reflected on what he had done:

> . . . with my equipment I would not have exceeded a 500 copy edition of 16 pages each if I had been wise, and on the open market deeper thoughts on costing would be necessary.

In 1967 he published the first poetry pamphlet under the imprint of Poet & Printer. This was *The Sermon*, by Peter Redgrove, in an edition of 500 copies. Since then he has issued nearly forty pamphlets at the rate of more than three new titles each year. His poets have included: Christopher Logue, Ted Hughes, Michael Longley, Penelope Shuttle, Robert Shaw and Alan Tucker.

Alan Tarling has become widely known in the last twelve years as a reliable publisher who loves poetry. He is able to choose the poets he wants to publish from among the famous or from the not so famous and occasionally he finds that he has to reject the famous name in favour of the new poet. He insists that he will only publish poetry that moves him.

Chapter eleven

THE PLOUGH PRESS

The Plough Press at Loughborough in Leicestershire was never part of the private press movement that revoled around Rigby Graham. Geoffrey Wakeman is a specialist private printer and publisher in his spare time, and he does not regard himself as belonging to any group at all. He was taught the art of hand-printing by Philip Gaskell at the College Press in Glasgow. Founded in 1967, the Plough Press prints and publishes books on printing history and paper making. It is Geoffrey Wakeman's intention to produce books containing 'important factual information' which can only be made by hand, but it has sometimes been necessary to vary this policy and have the printing and binding of his more complicated productions done by commercial firms. A great deal of work is put into each book from the press; Geoffrey Wakeman expects a financial return for the research, the writing, designing and printing he has undertaken. In addition to the intellectual input, the books have in the past required a capital investment of between £600 and £700 for materials and distribution. Most books from the press are taken up by American booksellers on behalf of specialist collectors in the USA. Some have been priced below £5 but recently his books have tended to be priced at between £15 and £50. The Plough Press possess a small Albion and a late nineteenth century Golding Pearl treadle press. The former has been used for pulling proofs and printing prospectuses, while the treadle press has been used to print most of his books.

The name of the press was derived from its first book *Share of Ploughs*, (1968). Roderick Cave had brought a collection of old electros depicting ploughs from Trinidad to Loughborough, and Geoffrey Wakeman decided he wanted to print them with accompanying verses set in Monotype Bembo. In the previous year Thomas Rae had printed *Anaglyptography* for the press and this had been the first book to appear under the Grian-aig imprint. Several humorous productions have come from the press, including *Law & ordure* (1969) and *Loughborough marble* (1971) which contained what appeared to be five specimens from a supposed local paper marbling industry.

English hand made papers suitable for bookwork (1972) earned Geoffrey Wakeman an international reputation. It included all the different varieties of hand-made papers which could be used for producing books and which could be easily obtained in 1972. Samples were printed with texts and illustrations of the processes involved in the making of paper by hand. A recent book from the press was, on this occasion, a serious study on marbling, *English marbled papers a documentary history* (1978), in an edition of 112 copies, containing results of an enquiry into the literature of English marbling together with twenty-six original samples, which were inserted by hand, from the classic patterns up to the most recent developments. Two of the samples are original nineteenth century papers. The text is printed in Garamond and Palatino on mould-made paper and quarter-bound in leather. Although Geoffrey Wakeman had to have most of the production work done by commercial firms, this book does meet his criterion of only publishing books which would not be practicable for a commercial publisher.

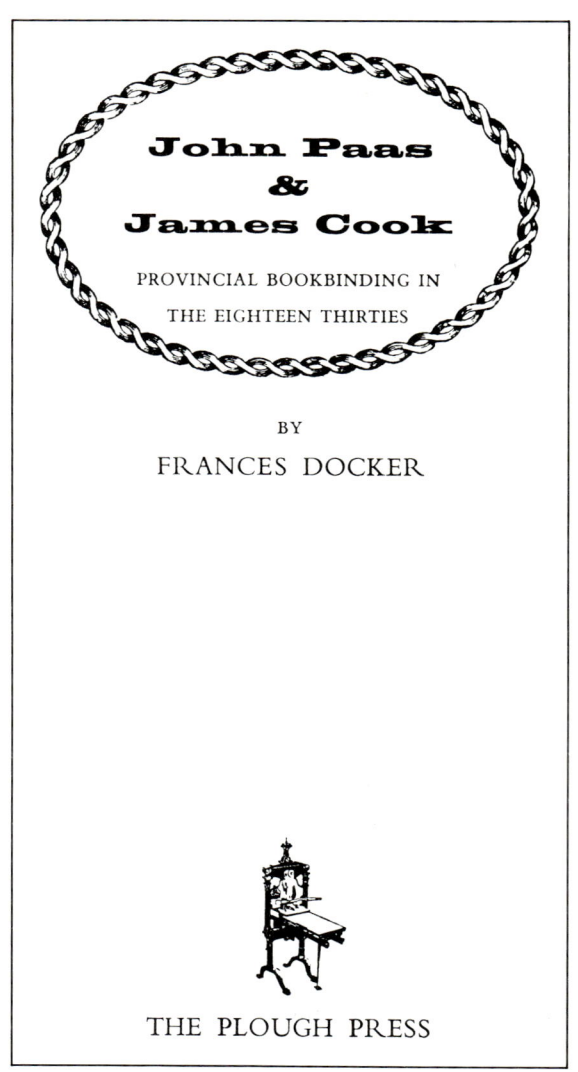

John Paas & James Cook. *Provincial bookbinding in the eighteen thirties*. Printed by Geoffrey Wakeman, The Plough Press. Title page.

Chapter twelve

THE MANDEVILLE PRESS

Peter Scupham is a poet who in partnership with another, John Mole, has printed and published poetry at the Mandeville Press in Hitchin for other poets, since 1974. Prior to the establishment of the press he was having difficulty establishing himself as a poet—the major publishers did not seem interested in his work. Then in 1972 he received an encouraging if severe letter, about poems he had once more submitted for publication, from an independent poetry publisher, Harry Chambers in Manchester. Chambers wrote stating that he practised Lord Reith's principle of dictatorship tempered by summary execution. He would only publish poems he liked and would return those he did not to the poet. *The small containers* (1972) came out in Chambers's Phoenix series of poetry pamphlets and was followed in the same year by *The snowing globe* in the same publisher's hardback series, Peterloo Poets. In 1973 Roy Lewis, at the Keepsake Press, issued a pamphlet of poetry *The Gift* for Peter Scupham, with four linocuts by Anthea Lawrence.

Although some of Scupham's own poetry has now been published by Oxford University Press, he continues to help other poets and publish some of their poetry at the Mandeville Press. He is by profession a teacher, by vocation a poet and by avocation a printer and publisher of poetry. This is not meant to imply that his part-time preoccupation with the publication of poetry pamphlets is in any way haphazard— far from it. After meeting Roy Lewis in 1973, he discussed the possibility of producing poetry in this way with Roger Burford Mason and John Mole. Deciding on a joint venture, they planned a series of poetry pamphlets, each containing a single poem with an accompanying illustration, along similar lines to the Keepsake poems of Roy Lewis. These became the 'Cellar Press Poets' issued by the Cellar Press in Hitchin. Once this project was under way and Peter Scupham felt he had gained enough experience, he founded the Mandeville Press, where he was joined by John Mole.

Unlike Alan Tarling, Peter Scupham does not pay his poets any royalty on sales. He justifies this by explaining that in its first five years the press has run at a loss. Eventually it will be 'in the black' and he admits that his policy may then have to be altered.

Inevitably when two poets set out to publish poetry there is going to be a family resemblance in what they publish. Peter Scupham, describing what he calls their 'concealed manifesto', explains that everything published by Mandeville falls within an English formalist tradition that is best represented among contemporary poets in the work of R S Thomas, James Reeves, Peter Porter and Anthony Thwaite. He goes on to characterize his own work and that of the Mandeville poets as the 'quiet voice of English poetry', which he regards as being undemonstrative, clear and exact and distanced from its subject. In selecting poetry for publication, a course is steered between the 'I went for a walk down a country lane' finicky landscape adulation and the barbarism of the 'bomb culture' declamation.

Shying away from the label 'private press', he prefers to think of Mandeville as a small poetry publishing house. He feels that the expensive private press book is not suited to the 'honest presentation' of poetry in the way that a commercially produced hardback book or small pamphlet can be. In designing a pamphlet he tries to produce something that advertizes its origin, using type, paper for the text and card for the cover to create an easily recognizable identity for the press. What he does not want is a finished product that looks too much like a professional publishing job.

Mandeville has a Model Three platen press and two treadle presses on which to print pamphlets in editions of 300 to 400 copies. These are sold mainly by subscription and through one or two bookshops, including the Basilisk Bookshop owned by Charlene Garry. Peter Scupham also takes pamphlets with him to poetry readings and sells a few copies to the audience on each occasion. All the time he is trying to establish personal contact with his customers because he feels that in the long run this is the only way to maintain an acceptable level of sales. Otherwise he claims he does not really know where the orders come from, except that they continue to reach him in almost every post. Each title from the press includes thirty-five copies which have been signed by the poet to cater for the collectors. The bulk of each edition is, he hopes, sold to poetry readers. The first pamphlet from the press was *Last Fruit* (1974) by Andrew Waterman. However it was not until the following year that the first illustrated production, *Two boys and a girl, playing in a churchyard* by Martin Booth, with a linocut by Margaret Stewart, was published, but since then most pamphlets have contained illustrations complementing the text; and a pleasing relationship between the two has become one of their most attractive features.

Several of the poets first published by Mandeville have since had work issued by commercial publishers. Andrew Waterman has appeared with Marvell Press, Freda Downie with Secker and Warburg, and Neil Powell with Caranet Press. This is something Peter Scupham would like to see repeated, because his intention when starting the press had been to provide the initial stepping stone for new poets.

THROUGH A GLASS DARKLY

Through every pane of this window's bubbled, uneven glass
we look down on a different country.
At each frontier a traveller
instantly conforms.

In one, everybody's important, a giant; in another, a dwarf.
One's all water — in that silky, forty-fathom swell
a swimmer goes by as a constantly nodding head
or a rhythmically protesting hand.

Crossing the vertical flaw in the next nation
when the sun's out, a man can disappear,
vanishing through a door painted indigo,
orange or violet in glowing, new-minted colours.

In shadow the same tall, knife-edge line
bites and splits him. Two men,
both dark, both identical, go by:
no telling which one to believe in.

To reach our front door any of our friends
must pass through half-a-dozen such States,
changing till we don't know who he really is,
or what he's made of us, the glass gods upstairs.

What you see from up here, or from down there,
depends on your mood,
and on the weather of the moment; most of all
on where you happen to be standing.

Water Lane, poems by Katherine Middleton. Printed by Peter Scupham, The Mandeville Press. Opening containing poem 'Through a glass darkly' and illustration by Mary Norman.

Chapter thirteen

THE BASILISK PRESS AND BOOKSHOP

The Basilisk Press and Bookshop in Hampstead is unique in the private press movement. Not only is Charlene Garry in business to publish fine books, but by opening a bookshop 'to bring all the presses under one roof', she has also created a thriving business centre, that is focusing the attention of even the most unworldly of private printers on the possibility of actually selling books to the general public.

Founded in 1974 the press itself has become a very successful undertaking. It publishes books in luxurious limited editions which require a level of capital investment that is beyond the reach of nearly every other contemporary private printer. While admitting that no private press today is capable of being as good as Kelmscott or Doves, Charlene Garry nevertheless sets out to produce facsimile editions of fine books which come as close as possible to their standards. The first production from Basilisk took the form of a very profitable homage to William Morris. *The Kelmscott Chaucer* (1974) was a handsome facsimile of his most successful venture. A previously unused fabric design by Morris was rediscovered and Liberty's of Regent Street reproduced it in linen for the binding. Published as a companion volume at the same time was a book of Edward Burne-Jones's pencil drawings, from which the original wood engravings had been made for Morris's *Chaucer*. The two books were issued in an edition of 500 sets which sold at £250 each.

With the press successfully established, Charlene Garry was able to produce other facsimile books. One important aspect of her policy has been to issue previously unpublished material from the eighteenth and nineteenth centuries relating to botanical and horticultural subjects. Only 'material that can be printed so accurately that it is virtually indistinguishable from the original' has been published by the press. She does the research for these productions, commissions artists and writers, and designs books herself, but all printing, plate-making and binding is placed with the best available commercial firms. Of the works that have appeared so far, probably the best is *Tulips and Tulipomania* (1977 by Wilfrid Blunt, with colour illustrations by Rory McEwan. The illustrations depicting the tulips, which come in a separate portfolio as well as appearing in the book, must be among the most exquisite representations of flowers ever painted. Authenticity is at the heart of what Charlene Garry is trying to achieve, authenticity carried as far as having paper made to the precise mix of the original pulp. If this and similar exact re-creations are not possible, she abandons the project and looks for a more tractable original. The books which have been published have each required a considerable financial investment, before any sales can be made to customers. However they have all been very profitable and a proportion of the return on the investment has been used to finance the bookshop.

Originally Charlene Garry rented only two rooms in the building the press and bookshop now occupy, but when an opportunity came to acquire the lease she bought it. The ground floor was redecorated and equipped as a bookshop. Many of the items stocked are only available through Basilisk or from the printers and publishers, because no other retail outlets handle them. This is particularly true of the cheaper pamphlets, posters and cards. A very wide range of current private press output is stocked, rising in price from 10p to £500. The presses such as Rainbow, Tern and World's End selling books to the higher end of the market (£50-£500) are well represented. The middle market range (£10-£50) is catered for by Rampant Lions, Plough and Scolar, among others, and the customer who is only interested in pamphlets and ephemera, usually priced at £2 or under has a very wide choice indeed. Not being particularly respectful of boundaries, Charlene Garry has also managed to obtain a small selection of 'little press' material which is as well displayed as any item in the shop. The best selling material comes from the natural history catagory, although in terms of numbers of titles on the shelves poetry books and pamphlets predominate. The general public makes good use of the shop, and customers often stay behind to browse and buy something after first being disappointed at not being able to purchase a dictionary or other conventional bookshop item.

To ensure that the widest possible range of private press publications can be stocked, books and other items are obtained from the presses on a sale or return basis, because Charlene Garry does not have the capital available to buy stock and finance her own fine editions at the same time. The printers themselves all seem satisfied with the arrangement, possibly because they are very well looked after by Basilisk. Every month each printer receives a cheque in payment of sales made of his publications, together with orders for any further copies which may be required. Extending opportunities for sales even further is the *Basilisk Press and Bookshop Catalogue 1*, a handsome paperback which was published in late 1978, priced £2.50. Only books costing more than £5 are described, but the publications of more than 100 private presses and independent publishers are listed, and there is a useful subject index. The success of the Basilisk Press and Bookshop is a welcome augury for the future of private printing in England.

Part three

A MARKET AND ITS PROSPECTS

Chapter fourteen

REACHING THE CUSTOMER

Private presses print and publish books in small editions. Rarely does the largest exceed 500 copies and usually they are limited to no more than 200 copies at a time, but there are some presses which do not even reach this level. Morris Cox at Gogmagog never issues more than a few dozen copies of his splendid productions, not from any wish to create a condition of artificial rarity for his work, but because of the extraordinary labour involved in making just a single copy of one of his books. Produced in such small editions, it hardly seems worth anyone paying serious attention to the marketing and distribution of these books and pamphlets, but as Samuel Johnson declared:

> There is nothing, Sir, too little for so little a creature as man. It is by studying little things that we attain the great art of having as little misery and as much happiness as possible.

Most private printers enjoy their printing and give free rein to their personal preferences. Their productions are idiosyncratic and normally do not conform to any conventional standards. In this lies their appeal for the people who buy their work. Once the private printer has decided to go beyond the stage of giving away the things he prints to friends and other printers, he begins building up a mailing list and hopes by doing so to attract a hard core of customers who will buy copies of everything he publishes. This leads on to the next stage; because when a printer has established a faithful following he may seek to guarantee their continuing loyalty by asking them to subscribe in advance for his books. The Mandeville Press of Peter Scupham has been very successful in this way and now sells a significant number of copies of each poetry pamphlet to regular subscribers. The printer-publishers of specialized books, similar to those of Geoffrey Wakeman at the Plough Press, often go to a lot of trouble to find booksellers who deal in their subjects and sell to otherwise inaccessible customers overseas. Serious collectors, both those who specialize in particular printing for itself and those who specialize in particular subjects, have little difficulty discovering the presses which might be useful to them from sources such as *Private Press Books* and the *Basilisk Press and Bookshop Catalogue*, and subsequently having themselves placed on the necessary mailing and subscription lists.

The ordinary customer does not appear to be catered for at all, but Alan Tarling at Poet & Printer sells between 400 and 500 copies of every pamphlet he issues, and only 150 of these are purchased by regular subscribers. The only advertisement he obtains is from the pamphlets he sells. Satisfied customers tell their friends and, in praising his work, help to increase sales and sustain the market for his products. Word of mouth, bearing favourable comment, is the surest way to establish demand for anything anyone wishes to sell, and this is particularly true for books because they are bought not out of need, but for reasons of self-gratification. However this has severe limitations for both the book-buyer and the printer. Both would be better served if the output of the private presses could be effectively distributed over the whole country and sold through general booksellers.

The Arts Council, through its literature officers in the Regional Arts Associations, has discussed ways of solving this problem with writers, printers and other interested parties. The proposal for a solution which emerged from these talks involved the establishment of a subsidised central distribution centre for English poetry and 'little press' books at an annual cost of approximately £40,000. Eventually the establishment of an 'English Poetry Council' is envisaged which would, with Arts Council support, encourage the publication, sale and reading of poetry in Great Britain.

A commercial alternative to these proposals is already operating successfully in Buckinghamshire. Ralph McBride, an American who developed the City Lights pocket poets series in San Francisco, has rented a disused chapel in Great Horwood. He uses this as a warehouse and distribution centre for books from more than thirty publishers, mostly 'small presses' in America. He employs one full-time representative for England and Ireland and hires the services of two freelance representatives on the continent, covering London himself. In only a few years he has built up a successful business with an annual turnover of more than £50,000.

The Arts Council proposal would probably succeed if it proved possible to recruit an energetic manager to run the distribution centre, but public funding is contrary to the spirit of the private press; the latter's origins lie deep within the individual printer who has an urge to create something which is unique. A better solution would probably be to combine something similar to Ralph McBride's operation with Charlene Garry's Basilisk Bookshop. The bookshop in Hampstead could provide the ideal base for freelance trade representation. It would be an uphill task for the representatives, because as Julia Horsfall claims:

> . . . elementary market research on the floor of the Basilisk shop proves beyond doubt that resistance to the small press publications comes not from the customer but from the booksellers.

The Other Planet

and three other fables

by ROY FULLER

with four wood engravings by
PAUL PETER PIECH

THE KEEPSAKE PRESS

The other planet, printed by Roy Lewis, Keepsake Press. Title page.

Booksellers are often suspicious of pamphlets. They do not usually sell quickly enough, the returns are not large and they are easily stolen. They would also object to the more expensive productions from private presses, because of the problem of finding money to buy such items for stock. This seems an overwhelming series of obstacles. Nonetheless it should be possible, given enthusiastic representation, to persuade a few booksellers to sell private press publications, thereby increasing the awareness of the general public, which in turn would be reflected in increased demand.

There is no danger that an effective marketing and distribution centre would destroy the private presses. Some, like Alan Tarling, would join in with great enthusiasm, others, like Geoffrey Wakeman, would probably ignore it and continue with their established publishing routine, while those who simply did not like it would withdraw, change the names of their presses and revert to giving away their publications. This last strategy is open to all private presses that might be faced with straightened or otherwise impossible circumstances. Their very smallness gives them great resilance and flexibility, qualities very necessary to their continued survival in a changing world.

Bibliography

ASSOCIATION OF LITTLE PRESSES *Catalogue of little press books in print . . . published in the United Kingdom* ALP 1970 : 1974 : 1977 : 1978.

BASILISK PRESS & BOOKSHOP *Catalogue 1* Basilisk Press and Bookshop, 1978.

Lists private press publications costing more than £5 each in the bookshop's stock.

CATALOGUE OF AN EXHIBITION OF BOOKS AND PRINTED EPHEMERA FROM TWENTY-EIGHT CONTEMPORARY PRIVATE PRESSES 3 December 1976–12 January 1977 at Swiss Cottage Library 1976.

ENGLISH PRIVATE PRESSES 1757-1961: catalogue of an exhibition 12–22 April 1961 The Times Bookshop, 1961.

Lists the books from 95 presses, displayed in the exhibition.

THE LITTLE PRESS MOVEMENT IN ENGLAND AND AMERICA. Catalogue. An exhibition held at the American Embassy 24 April to 24 May 1968 Turret Books, 1968.

THE PAGE RIGHT PRINTED: An exhibition of the work of the private presses from William Morris to the present day Glasgow School of Art 1-12 May 1973.

Lists the books from 43 presses, displayed in the exhibition.

POETRY INFORMATION Peter Hodgkiss c/o 18 Clairview Road London SW16 1970–issued twice each year.

'Publications received' section lists the current output of the 'little presses'.

PRIVATE LIBRARIES ASSOCIATION *Private Press Books 1959*–annual PLA 1960–

Lists the output of private presses in Great Britain, Europe, USA, and elsewhere. Part three lists 'Literature of private printing'

RANSOM, W *Private presses and their books, 1929* Reprinted by Philip C Duschnes, 1963.
The bibliography is a comprehensive listing of the books of older private presses in Great Britain and the USA.
Selective checklists of press books 1945-1950 Reprinted in one volume by Philip C Duschnes 1963
RIDLER, W *British modern press books, a descriptive checklist of unrecorded items* Covent Garden Press, 1971.
Lists items not included in Ransom, Tomkinson and *Private press books.*
STANDING, J *The private press today* Brewhouse Press, 1967.
Two editions: 24pp and 32pp, were issued of this catalogue of the private press exhibition held at the 17th King's Lynn Festival.
TOMKINSON, G S *A select bibliography of the principal modern presses, public and private in Great Britain and Ireland* First Edition Club, 1928.
The standard bibliography.

GENERAL WORKS AND HISTORIES OF THE
PRIVATE PRESSES
CAVE, R *The Private Press* Faber, 1971.
A general history: the fifteenth century to the late 1960s.
The Private Press: handbook to an exhibition held in the School of Librarianship 6–11 May 1968 Loughborough Technical College, 1968.
FRANKLIN, C *The Private Presses* Studio Vista, 1969.
An account of the English private press movement.
GLAISTER G A *Glossary of the Book: terms used in papermaking, printing, bookbinding and publishing, with notes on illuminated manuscripts, bibliophiles, private presses and printing societies* Allen & Unwin, 1960.

Appendix C. John Ryder 'The contemporary private press' which is a description of Ryder's classification of private presses.
McLEAN, R *Modern book design from William Morris to the present day* Faber, 1958.
RANSOM, W *Private presses and their books 1929* (Reprinted by Philip C Duschnes 1963)
Contains a useful analysis of different definitions of private presses.

ORIGINS
BLAND, D 'The Perpetua Press' *The Private Library* second series 3(2) 1970 78-90
'The Perpetua Press: a checklist' 87-90.
COOPER, A C 'Notes on the printing methods of the Golden Cockerel Press' *The Private Library* 4(3) July 1962 38-40.
KEYNES, G *A study of the illuminated books of William Blake - poet, printer, prophet* Methuen, with Trianon Press, Paris, 1965.
MOSLEY, J 'The press in the parlour: some notes on the amateur printer and his equipment' *The Black Art* 2(1) Spring 1963 2-16.
TURNER, G *The Private Press, its achievement and influence* Association of Assistant Librarians, Midland Division, 1954.
Describes aims and achievements of the Kelmscott, Doves, Essex House, Ashendene, Golden Cockerel, Gregynog and Nonesuch presses.

SURVIVAL AND REVIVAL
BAKER, A 'The Quest for Guido' *The Private Library* second series 2(4) 1969 138-176.
BROWN, P A H and BAKER, A 'The Latin Press: a tentaive checklist' *The Private Library* second series 2(4) 1969 180-187.

CARTER, W 'Rampant Lion' *The Private Library* 5(3) July 1964 42-44.

CAVE, R 'Blake's Mantel: a memoir of Ralph Chubb' *Book Design and Production* 3(2) Summer 1960 24-28.

'Why Potocki? ' *The Private Library* 8(1) Spring 1967 6-8.

DREYFUS, J 'The Vine Press' *The Private Library* 7(2) Summer 1966 40-44.

Notes on production of Vine Press Books, by John Peters 42-44.

ECKERT, R P 'James Guthrie and the Pear Tree Press' *The American Book Collector* 13 (9/10) Summer 1963 13-33.

FAIRFAX HALL, B 'The Stourton Press (from 1930-1935) *The Private Library* second series 2(2) 1969 54-67.

Checklist of books printed at the Stourton Press 61-62.

FARLEIGH, J *The creative craftsman* G Bell and Sons, 1950 231-240 Guido Morris: Job printer, St Ives.

'The Folio Society' (unsigned) *Private Libraries Association Quarterly* 1(5) January 1958 54-58.

FRANKLIN, C 'James Guthrie' *The Private Library* second series 9(1) 1976 2-18.

GRAHAM, R 'Potocki' *The Private Library* 8(1) Spring 1967 8-26.

A tentative checklist of the work of Geoffrey, Count Potocki 23-26.

GUTHRIE, F 'Books from the hand of James Joshua Guthrie' *The Private Library* second series 9(1) 1976 44-47.

GUTHRIE, J 'The hand printer and his work'. *The Private Library* second series 9(1) 1976 24-43.

A reprint of a paper read at the Double Crown Club in 1934.

GUY, P 'Twenty five years of the Folio Society' *Penrose Annual* 66 1973 63-76.

'The Influence of the Folio Society' (unsigned) *Book Design and Production* 7(2) Summer 1964 106-115.

LISTER, R 'The Golden Head Press' *The Private Library* 5(4) October 1964 62-69.
Checklist of Golden Head Press books 65-69.
MORAN, J 'The Vine Press' *Book Design and Production* 3(3) 1960 50-54.
REID, A 'Ralph Chubb, the unknown: his life 1892-1960 *The Private Library* second series 3(3) Autumn 1970 141-156.
'Ralph Chubb, the unknown: his work' *The Private Library* second series 3(4) Winter 1970 193-213.
SANDFORD, C 'Press Book Production 1945-52' *Penrose Annual* 47 1953 31-34.
'Sebastian Carter' (unsigned) *Book Design and Production* 3(4) 1960 46-47.
TARLING, A *Will Carter, printer: an illustrated study* The Galahad Press, 1968.
THOMAS, E 'James Guthrie' *The Private Library* second series 9(1) 1976 19-23.
WARD, P 'The Vine "Parliament of Women" ' *The Private Library* 3(6) April 1961 81-82.
'Will Carter, Printer' (unsigned) *Book Design and Production* 2(2) 1959 28-36.

A NEW MOVEMENT
CAVE, R and RAE, T 'Contemporary pressbook design'. In 'Private Press Books' 1959 1-5 PLA. 1960.
CAVE, R 'Gogmagog: the private press of Morris Cox' *The American Book Collector* 12(9) May 1962 20-23.
'Printing at the Brewhouse' *The American Book Collector* 16(9) May 1966 18-24.
'The private press and the public library' *Library Association Record* 63(7) July 1961 246-247.
'The Signet Press' *The Private Library* 3(5) January 1961 58-59.

'Thomas Rae: a modern Scottish printer' *The American Book Collector* 12(2) 1961 18-21.
'The work of the private press' *British Book News* December 1960 839-843.
'The work of the private press' *British Book News* December 1964 857-861.
CHAMBERS, D 'The Gogmagog Press' *The Private Library* 5(1) 1964 5-10.
'The Society of Private Printers' *The Private Library* 4(3) July 1962 47-48.
'The Society of Private Printers' *The Private Library* third series 1(2) Summer 1978 50-69.
GRAHAM, R 'The Orpheus Press' *The American Book Collector* 19(5) January 1969 11-22.
'The Pandora Press' *The Private Library* 7(1) Spring 1966 5-12.
ISAAC, P 'The Allenholme Press' *The Private Library* 4(4) October 1962 66-68.
MASON, J 'Adventurous papermaking: the founding of the Twelve by Eight Mill' *The Black Art* 2(3) Autumn 1963 74-78.
Papermaking as an artistic craft Faber, 1959: second edition, 1963.
'Twelve by Eight' *The Private Library* 2(3) January 1959 38-41.
A paper read at the Double Crown Club in 1958.
[MORAN, J] 'Raison d'Etre' *Book Design and Production* 1(1) Spring 1958 9-10.
An editorial outlining the policy of the journal.
MORRIS, A *The private press in Leicestershire* The Plough Press 1976.
PHILLIPS, J 'Private press revival' *Library Association Record* 68(5) May 1966 174-176.

RAE, T and HANDLEY-TAYLOR, G *The book of the private press, a checklist.* The Signet Press 1958.
Foreword by John Ryder.
RAE, T 'The Signet Press' *The Black Art* 1(3) Autumn 1962 86-90.
RYDER, J *A miniature folio of private presses* Minature Press 1960.
'Miniature folio of private presses 1960' *Book Design and Production* 3(3) 1960 25-30.
Including Ryder's criticisms of the printing in the original folio.
Printing for pleasure Bodley Head 1955: second edition 1976.
A suite of fleurons, or a preliminary enquiry into the history & combinable natures of certain printers flowers Phoenix House 1956.
Historical notes on the development and uses of printers ornaments.
TAYLOR, K 'The Ark Press' *The Private Library* 4(5) January 1963 90-94.

POETRY AND THE PRIVATE PRESS
BROWNJOHN, A 'Public poets and private presses' *The Author* 74(1) Spring 1968 25-27.
COTTON, J 'The Fantasy Poets' *The Private Library* second series 2(1) Spring 1967 3-13.
Checklist 10-13.
GRAHAM, R 'The Daedalus Press of Stoke Ferry' *Private Printer & Private Press* (1) February 1968 7-20.
Checklist 19-20.
'Avant-Garde poetry from the Stone Turret' *The American Book Collector* 24(3) January-February 1974 12-26.
'Transican Books: a fragile experiment, a poet's printing press' *The American Book Collector* 24(6) July-August 1974 12-15.

MELLOR, O 'The Fantasy Press' *Private Printer & Private Press* 1(1) February 1968 33-38.
MILLS, S 'Concrete Poetry' *The Private Library* second series 2(3) Autumn 1969 95-106.
ROLPH, J 'Some notes on the Scorpion Press' *The Private Library* second series 4(4) Winter 1971 156-164.
Chronological checklist of Scorpion Press Books 162-164.
'The Scorpion Press' (unsigned) *Book Design and Production* 2(4) 1959 34-35.

A LIVING TRADITION
BENN, E 'Setting up a new life in an old fashioned type . . . ' *The Daily Telegraph* September 13 1978.
CAVE, R 'The work of the private presses' *British Book News* August 1970 581-584.
CHAMBERS, D 'Printing for pleasure' *Times Literary Supplement* September 15 1978 1024.
FIELD, J 'Power to the presses' *Financial Times* January 20 1979.
FISCHER FELDMAN, J 'A Brewhouse Press exhibition in America' *The Private Library* second series 7(1) Spring 1974 34-37.
GRAHAM, R 'Icarus over England' *The American Book Collector* 18(5-6) January-February 1968 14-25.
An account of the private press exhibition held at the 17th King's Lynn Festival, July 22-29 1967.
'International private press exhibition, Loughborough 1968' *The American Book Collector* 19(2) October 1968 8-17.
A description of 'The private press', an exhibition held in the School of Librarianship, Loughborough May 6-11 1968.
GRAHAM, R 'The page right printed' *The American Book Collector* 24(4) March-April 1974 10-20.
An account of a private press exhibition held in Glasgow 1-12 May 1973.

'Paul Peter Piech and the Taurus Press of Willow Dene' *The American Book Collector* 20(6) March-April 1970 30-35.,
Checklist of Taurus Press publications 35.,
GRAHAM, R and WILLOUGHBY, M 'A tale of two cities: a note on the private press exhibition at Watford 1970 *The American Book Collector* 21(6) March-April 1971 19-36.
HARDACRE, K 'The private press in Hertfordshire'.
An address delivered at the opening of an exhibition in the Central Library Watford September 3 1969.
'The private press of Paul Piech' *Penrose Annual* 69 1976 98-112.
'Private presses—private pleasures' *British Printer* 89(8) August 1976 25-27.
KLEINMAN, P 'Private press gang: Small independent private presses' *Sunday Times Magazine* March 12 1978 14-15.
[LEWIS, R] 'Outside the whale' *Times literary supplement* November 18 1965 1023.
A brief account of the contemporary private press movement.
MORAN, J 'Private presses and the printing industry' *British Printer* 85(4) April 1962 105-120.
NEWPORT, B 'The small press movement in Britain' *Antiquarian Book Monthly Review* 4(6) June 1977 240-246.
OGG, J 'Alternative fiction publishing—frail but vital' *Assistant Librarian* October 1978 111-114.
PRYOR, L A 'Printing machines used by private presses, 1962-9'. In 'Private Press Books' 1970 ix-xiii PLA, 1971.
STANDING, J 'The private press today—an exhibition' *The Private Library* 8(3) Autumn 1967 63-66.
An Account of the private press exhibition held at the 17th King's Lynn Festival July 22-29 1967.
STRACHAN, W J 'A new private press: The World's End Press' *The Private Library* second series 5(2) Summer 1972 84-87.

The task of the private press; marginal books and improving standards (unsigned) *Times Literary Supplement* April 26 1963, 294.
A brief historical survey examining the reasons for the establishment of private presses since the fifteenth century.

THE CUCKOO HILL PRESS
CHAMBERS, D 'The Cuckoo Hill Press' *The Private Library* 4(6) April 1963 110-114.
The Cuckoo Hill Press (unsigned) *The Black Art* 1(1) Spring 1962 17-19.
RYDER, J 'A note on the Cuckoo Hill Press, Pinner' *Book Design and Production* 3(2) Summer 1960 15.

THE SHOESTRING PRESS
TARLING, A 'The Shoestring Press' *Small Printer* January 1967 5-8.

THE KEEPSAKE PRESS
CAVE, R 'The Keepsake Press of Roy Lewis and daughters' *The American Book Collector* 14(7) March 1964 10-14.
Checklist of the publications of the Keepsake Press 14.
LEWIS, R 'The Keepsake Press' *The Private Library* 4(7) July 1963 127-130.

THE KIT-CAT PRESS
HARDACRE, K 'Printer's pleasure' *Small Printer* January 1965 7-11.

POET & PRINTER
COTTON, J 'The Poet and Printer Press: some notes and a checklist' *The Private Library* second series 4(3) Autumn 1971 128-139.
Checklist of Poet & Printer publications 132-139.

TARLING, A 'Absolute beginner' *Small Printer* August 1965 10-12.
'Binding at a little press' *Small Printer* January 1969 14-16.

THE PLOUGH PRESS
MORRIS, A *The private press in Leicestershire* The Plough Press, 1976. pp31-32 Plough Press.

THE MANDEVILLE PRESS
BURFORD MASON, R 'The Mandeville Press of Hitchin' *The Private Library* second series 10(1) Spring 1977 22-34. Checklist of Mandeville Press Publications 26-34.

THE BASILISK PRESS AND BOOKSHOP
NEWPORT, B 'The Basilisk Bookshop, or bargains for all' *Antiquarian Book Monthly Review* 6(2) February 1979 64-67.

REACHING THE CUSTOMER
HORSFALL, J 'Notes on the small presses in Britain' *British Book News* September 1978 677-681.
LANDESMAN, J 'A site for small presses' *Bookseller* September 2 1978 p1965.
An account of Ralph McBride's distribution centre for American 'small presses'.
Little Press & poetry distribution Greater London Arts Association April 1977.
Discussion Paper for private circulation.
OGG, J 'Alternative fiction publishing—frail but vital' *Assistant Librarian* October 1978 111-114.

Appendix
Selective Checklists of 'Eight Contemporary Presses'

INTRODUCTION
The following checklists are as complete as it has been possible to make them at the time of going to press. Because private press books are issued in such small editions, and because a considerable proportion of their output is ephemeral, it is difficult to ensure comprehensiveness. When they are available 'Private Press Books' serial numbers (PPB 77.246) and 'Basilisk Press and Bookshop Catalogue 1' references (Basilisk Catalogue 1 p10) are given at the end of an entry to indicate where a more detailed bibliographical description is available.

BASILISK PRESS AND BOOKSHOP
THE KELMSCOTT CHAUCER in facsimile. With a companion volume containing Edward Burne-Jones's previously unpublished pencil drawings for the wood engravings.
566pp & 192pp   500 copies   1974   Price £250
THE AUSTRALIAN FLOWER PAINTINGS OF FERDINAND BAUR in facsimile by Dr William T Stearn and Wilfrid Blunt. 25 plates printed in ten colour lithography.
128pp   500 numbered copies   1976   Price £420   Basilisk Catalogue 1 p9
THE RED BOOKS OF HUMPHRY REPTON by Edward Malins. Four volumes of varying size. Collotype facsimiles of Red Books painted between 1792-1812.
500 numbered sets   1977   Price £495   Basilisk Catalogue 1 p11

TULIPS AND TULIPOMANIA by Wilfrid Blunt, illustrated by Rory McEwen. Portfolio containing 100pp book and 8 separate prints of boldly coloured tulips.
500 numbered copies   1977   Price £295; book alone £75 prints £35 each   Basilisk Catalogue 1 p12
GARDENS OF DELIGHT, THE ROCOCO ENGLISH LANDSCAPE OF THOMAS ROBINS THE ELDER by John Harris. Two volumes printed by Lund Humphries. Vol 1 120 illustrations in colour, text in sepia 76pp; Vol II 15 plates in eight colour lithography.
46pp   500 numbered copies   1978   Price £435   Basilisk Catalogue 1 p10

THE CUCKOO HILL PRESS
HERE'S ROSEMARY. Poems selected from 'The language and sentiment of flowers'. Three wood engravings by David Chambers.
21pp   2 copies on Japanese white paper   6 copies on Japanese vellum
33 copies on Basingwerk Parchment   1959.   All copies distributed to friends of the printer PPB 59.13
SOME DECORATIVE JAPANESE PAPERS. A folder designed and produced by David Chambers for the PLA Society of Private Printers.
16pp   41 copies   1960   Not for sale PPB 60.16
SOME DECORATIVE JAPANESE PAPERS.
28pp   59 copies   2nd edition 1960.   Not for sale PPB 61.19
THE OFFICE PRESS: an account of its construction by David Chambers with three line illustrations.
15pp   27 copies   1961   Price 7s   PPB 61.20
ELIZABETH II NUMISMATA: 13 prints made from coins of the reign of Elizabeth II. With a note by David Chambers.
19 leaves French folded   About 70 copies   1964.   Not for sale PPB 64.27

THE APOSTLES' CREED. With 15 wood engravings by Philip Ross.
20pp   84 copies   1966   Price £2 2s   PPB 66.35
SOME NINETEENTH CENTURY TRADE CARDS & LABELS. Nine Prints taken from the original copper plates.
17 leaves   44 copies   1966/7   Not for sale   PPB 67.87
FOUR ENGRAVINGS ON WOOD. Cut by Thomas Bewick, Charlton Nesbit, John Bewick & Luke Clennell for G L Way's 'Fabliaux' of Le Grand, printed by Bulmer in 1796 & 1800.
8 leaves French-folded   About 140 copies   1969   Not for sale   PPB 69.47
WOOD-ENGRAVINGS by T Sturge Moore.
Title-page + 71 prints   5 sets printed   1970   Not for sale   PPB 70.46
ENGRAVINGS ON WOOD by Thomas Bewick and his pupils from G L Way's edition of Le Grand's 'Fabliaux' 50 prints from the original wood-blocks.
54 leaves French-folded   16 copies   1969/71   Not for sale   PPB 71.61
MEILLERIE. Poems by Count Potocki of Montalk with a wood engraving by Mark Severin.
16pp   277 copies   1973   25 for sale price £10, 105 for sale price £3   PPB 73.42
AUTUMN LEAVES. Two fragments by Ralph Chubb, with 14 marginal drawings by the author.
24pp   39 copies   1975   Not for sale   PPB 75.66
CARACTERES DE L'IMPRIMERIE, NOUVELLEMENT GRAVE'S par S P Fournier le jeune, with 8 page note by David Chambers.
51 leaves   175 copies   1976   Price £8
ON PRINTING BY HAND. David Chambers.
Four leaves French-folded   300 copies   1977   Not for sale

THE KEEPSAKE PRESS

A FADED GARLAND OF FAMILY VERSE by C M E & R
12pp   36 copies   1957   unpriced

METAMORPHOSES. Poems by Edward Lowbury.
16pp   80 copies   1958   unpriced

PATRIXBOURNE.   Five country poems by Rose Marie Hodgson.
16pp   100 copies   1958   unpriced

THE DEATH OF GOD, A DREAM by Roy Lewis with decorative initials cut in lino by Elizabeth Lewis.
15pp   50 copies   1959   unpriced   PPB 59.36

WHITHER SHALL I WANDER?   A SHEAF OF SIX POEMS by Gordon Symes.
11pp   150 copies   1959   unpriced   PPB 59.37

AN OCTET OF VERSE by E St Olave.
12pp   75 copies   1960   unpriced   PPB 60.42

PURPLE GOLD MOUNTAIN. Poems from China, by Ahmed Ali.
16pp   175 copies   1960   unpriced   PPB 60.43

REMINISCENCES OF A TAX INSPECTOR by Charles St J Shores.
15pp   90 copies   1960   unpriced   PPB 60.44

REPORT AND ADIEUX by Roy Lewis.
8pp   about 200 copies   1961   Not for sale   PPB 62.58

SEVEN DAYS AND TWELVE THOUSAND MILLION YEARS OF CREATION. The first chapter of the book of Genesis. With linocut initials by Elizabeth Lewis.
6pp   40 copies printed for the PLA Society of Private Printers   1961   Not for sale   PPB 61.48

THE HISTORY OF ENGLAND by Miss Austen, with linocuts by Elizabeth Lewis.
23pp   75 copies   1962   Price 10s   PPB 62.60

POEMS IN INDIA by Francis Watson.
11pp   125 copies   1962   Price 6s   PPB 62.61

WAYSIDE FLOWERS by William Allingham.
16pp about 200 copies 1962 Not for sale PPB 62.59
FLOWERS & NON-FLOWERS by R L C Foottit with two linocuts by Helen Gleadow.
8pp 120 copies 1963 Not for sale PPB 63.62
OXFORD/LONDON/AMERICA. Poems by Ann Titmuss.
8pp 100 copies 1963 Not for sale PPB 63.61
THE SPIRIT & THE BODY an Orphic Poem, by Peter Russell.
9pp 220 copies 1963 Price 8s 6d PPB 63.63
A CHRONOLOGY OF WILLIAM SHAKESPEARE'S LIFE AND WORKS.
20pp About 200 copies [1964] Price 8s
LANDSCAPES. Poems by Camillo Pennati. Translated from the Italian by Peter Russell, with an introduction by Salvatore Quasimodo.
14pp 200 copies 1964 Price 8s 6d PPB 64.64
NON TANTUM NOMINE BARBARAE. A poem by Ian Headland.
8pp 120 copies 1964 Price 3s PPB 64.66
THROWAWAY LINES by Gavin Ewart, with five linocuts by Warwick Hutton.
14pp 200 copies 1964 Price 6s 6d PPB 64.65
NEW POEMS by Edward Lowbury.
16pp 180 copies 1965 Price 5s PPB 65.85
MOMENTS OF TRUTH. Nineteen short poems by living poets.
24pp 350 copies 1965 Price 5s PPB 65.87
POEMS AND DRAWINGS by Mervyn Peake, with five drawings in the text reproduced by photo-lithography, and one on the cover by silk-screen. Foreword by Maurice Collis.
13pp 150 copies 1965 75 copies for sale, Price 6s 6d PPB 65.86

FRONTIER MIDLANDS. Poems by Jennet Thomas with five linocuts by Tim Craven.
20pp   180 copies   1966   Price 5s   PPB 66.87
TWO CHILDREN. Poems by Gavin Ewart, with a wood-engraving by Prid Lasenby.
20pp   175 copies   1966   Price 6s 6d   PPB 66.86
CAPTAIN OF THE FLEET. The career of Admiral Sir William Domett, GCB, 1751-1828, by Captain A F P Lewis, CBE, RN(Ret).
ii, 32pp   100 copies   1967   Price 5s   PPB 67.78
THE HARLOT'S HOUSE by Oscar Wilde, with six stencilled illustrations (including those on the wrappers) by Daphne Lord.
4pp   40 copies   1967   25 copies for sale   Price 7s 6d   PPB 67.79
SOLEMN ADULTERY AT BREAKFAST CREEK. An Australian Ballad by Peter Porter, with three linocuts by Paul Peter Piech.
12pp   200 copies   1968   Price 7s 6d   PPB 68.71
CANNON HILL PARK. Three ballads by Don Collis, with four silk-screen illustrations by the author.
7pp   175 copies 1969   Price 5s   PPB 69.95
FIGURES OF EIGHT. Poems by Edward Lowbury, with nine illustrations by Bryan Brooke.
20pp   150 copies   1969   Price 6s   PPB 69.93
THE HORN: LE COR. A poem by Alfred de Vigny, with a white linocut by Elizabeth Lewis.
7pp   100 copies   1969   Price 7s 6d   PPB 69.94
LAST POEMS by Rose Marie Hodgson.
12pp   100 copies   1969   Not for sale   PPB 69.92
ALL RIGHT AUDEN, I KNOW YOU'RE THERE. A quick thought by Shirley Toulson.
7pp   75 copies   1970   Not for sale   PPB 70.121

CIRCUMCISION'S NOT SUCH A BAD THING AFTER ALL and other poems by Shirley Toulson.
24pp   175 copies   1970   25 copies signed by the author Price 8s, 150 copies Price 5s   PPB 70.91
TAPESTRY & ARCHITECTURE. An address by Maxwell Fry. With half-tone reproductions of two tapestries by Miriam Sacks.
8pp   250 copies   1970   50 copies for sale   Price 2s 6d   PPB 70.90
TRIP. A sequence of poems through the USA by John Brunner, linocuts by Paul Peter Piech.
33pp   200 copies   1971   50 copies signed by the author Price 60p   150 unsigned Price 40p   PPB 71.110
TWO BAKER'S DOZEN SUPERIOR QUALITY CLERIHEWS MADE FROM THE PUREST HISTORICAL PRECEDENTS by Walter Mee.
28pp   125 copies   1971   Price 8p   PPB 71.111
UNPUBLISHED POEMS & DRAFTS by James Elroy Flecker, with an introduction and brief notes by Martin Booth.
16pp   205 copies   1971   170 copies for sale   Price 45p   PPB 71.109
A WINNOWING OF SILENCE. Poems by Martin Booth, with two linocuts by Jennifer Carey.
21pp   180 copies   1971   Price 40p   PPB 71.108
THE FAULT DEAR BRUTUS. Sonnets by Shirley Toulson.
34pp   250 copies   1972   Price 40p   PPB 72.84
KEEPSAKE POEMS. A series of illustrated poems by various authors and artists. Each poem and its visual counterpart is hand-printed as a double-spread. Each edition is limited to 180 copies.
1972-   25p to 40p each   PPB 72.86
NO LAND IS WASTE, DR ELIOT by Jean Simmons.
24pp   300 copies   1972   Price 40p   PPB 72.85

THE GIFT. Poems by Peter Scupham, with four linocuts by Anthea Lawrence.
24pp   200 copies   1973   Price 40p   PPB 73.85
BSJ. A monody to the plan of Milton on the death by Suicide of B S Johnson in November 1973 by Alan Tucker.
12pp   125 copies   1974   100 copies for sale   Price 25p   PPB 74.62
CATS FREE AND FAMILIAR. Poems by Robert Leach with four woodcuts and woodcut lettering by Warwick Hutton.
16pp   185 copies   1974   Price 30p   PPB 74.61
THE AMERICAN WAR under the cover of Sir William Howe, by the Rev. Charles Wesley. Edited by Donald Baker with a half-tone reproduction of the Lily portrait.
36pp   260 copies   1975   75 copies bound in brown cloth with a linocut by Elizabeth Lewis Price £3.95, 185 copies bound in card, with same dust-jacket Price £1.95 PPB 75.111
ASPECTS OF PARIS by John Press with seven autholithographs by Gordon Bradshaw.
20pp   250 copies   1975   25 numbered copies signed by the author and artist Price 75p, 225 unsigned copies Price 35p PPB 75.110
THE PRACTICE OF PARLOUR PRINTING CONSIDERED AS A SPECIFIC AGAINST INSOMNIA & LIKE DISORDERS WITH A WARNING ON SIDE EFFECTS ILLUSTRATED BY A RETROSPECT OF THE ACTIVITIES OF THE KEEPSAKE PRESS FROM ITS FOUNDATON ... by Roy Lewis
12pp   130 copies   1975   For exchange with other private presses   Not for sale   PPB 75.112
POETRY AND PARADOX, AN ESSAY, WITH 19 RELEVANT POEMS by Edward Lowbury.
33pp   250 copies   1976   25 signed and numbered bound in cloth Price £2.75, 50 signed and numbered copies in paper wrappers Price £1.50, the remainder in paper covers Price 75p

THE SNOW QUEEN & OTHER POEMS. Hans Christian Anderson, translated by Anne Born.
16pp   185 copies   1976
A VERY PERSONAL NOTE ON THE RELATIONSHIP BETWEEN A PRIVATE PRESS AND PUBLISHING by Roy Lewis.
4pp   number of copies not given   1977   not priced
THE OTHER PLANET. Four fables by Roy Fuller with four wood engravings by Paul Peter Piech.
26pp   275 copies   1979   Price 90p
WOODS BEYOND A CORNFIELD by Stanley Cook with drawings by Rigby Graham.
28pp   220 copies   1979   Price 95p

THE KIT-CAT PRESS
POEMS Frederick Palmer 1958.
A LITTLE BOOK OF TYPE SPECIMENS
16pp   1959   gratis   PPB 59.39
LAST THINGS AND OTHER POEMS by Edward Pine.
21pp   160 copies   1962   Price 4s   PPB 62.62
TULIPS, STILTS AND BALLOONS by Peter Lyon, with a linocut by Eric Webb.
8pp   160 copies   1963   Not for sale   PPB 63.64
THREE TORTOISE POEMS. E V Rieu 1964
EDGAR & EMMA by Jane Austen.
17pp   about 250 copies   1967   Price 7s 6d   PPB 67.80
THE PRIVATE PRESS IN HERTFORDSHIRE by Kenneth Hardacre.
10pp   about 140 copies   1969: reprinted 1971   Price 10s   PPB 69.96
DAINTY DEVICES. A collection of printers' marks. Nine fingerprints of members of the London Chappel.
17pp   30 copies   1969   Not for sale   PPB 69.98

POEM IN OCTOBER by Dylan Thomas.
19pp   1 copy presented to the printer's daughter to mark her 21st birthday   1969   Not for sale   PPB 69.97
GREY AND GREEN. Poems by Janet Brice.
24pp about 250 copies   1970   about 150 copies for sale   Price 8s   PPB 70.92
TRAVELLING. A poem by Jeremy Robson, with line-block reproductions of three drawings by Kenneth Hardacre.
11pp   160 copies   1972   50 copies for sale   Price 50p   PPB 72.87
CONTINENTAL SKETCHES by Kenneth Hardacre, with line-block reproductions of five drawings by the author.
28pp about 100 copies   1973   Not for sale   PPB 73.87
THE MOWER AGAINST GARDENS by Andrew Marvell, with a line-block reproduction of a drawing by Frederick Palmer.
7pp   50 copies   1974   Price 45p   PPB 74.64
DAMON THE MOWER. Four poems by Andrew Marvell, with line-block reproductions of eight drawings by Frederick Palmer.
22pp   200 copies   1975   Price £1.70   PPB 75.115
EVEN CAXTON HAD HIS TROUBLES WITH THE PICKETS by Roy Lewis.
11pp   170 copies   1976   Price £1
THE GARDEN by Andrew Marvell.
8pp   200 copies   1976   Price 80p
INNER PERSUASIONS. Religious poems by Doris Pulsford.
24pp   120 copies   1976   Price £1.50
THE DAFFODIL. A short story by Carrie Noall.
10pp   180 copies   1977   Price 50p
FIVE POEMS by John Gohorry, illustration on title page by Colin Reeve.
12pp   (about 200 copies)   1977   Price 75p

OUT OF THE IVORY GATE by J B Priestley.
11pp   200 copies   1978   80p
TO HIS COY MISTRESS by Andrew Marvell, drawing on cover by Colin Reeve.
16pp   185 copies   1978   80p

THE MANDEVILLE PRESS
LAST FRUIT. Poems by Andrew Waterman.
11pp   130 copies   1974   30 signed copies   Price 50p   100 copies   Price 20p   PPB 75.134
NIGHT MUSIC. Poems by Freda Downie.
14pp   145 copies   1974   35 signed copies Price 50p, 110 copies Price 30p   PPB 75.135
THE CORRIDOR. Poems by C H Sisson.
14pp   230 copies   1975   30 signed copies Price 50p, 200 copies Price 30p   PPB 75.145
A FEW ROOKS CIRCLING TREES. Poems by Donald Ward.
21pp   174 copies   1975   39 signed copies Price 50p, 120 copies Price 30p   PPB 75.143
NINE MUSES. Poems by Freda Downie and eight other poets (Dragon cards, Series 1).
9 cards loosely inserted in envelope,   120 sets   1975   20 signed sets Price £1, 100 sets Price 30p   PPB 75.141
NINE MUSES, SERIES TWO. Poems by John Cotton and eight other poets (Dragon cards, Series 2).
9 cards loosely inserted in envelope,   120 sets   1975   20 signed sets Price £1, 100 sets Price 30p   PPB 75.141
PANTOMIME CAT. A poem by John Mole, with a line-block reproduction of a drawing by Carola Scupham.
2pp   145 copies   1975   25 signed copies Price 25p, 120 copies Price 10p
THE SHOOTING STAR. Poems by Trevor McMahon.
13pp   125 copies   1975   25 signed copies Price 50p, 80 copies Price 25p   PPB 75.138

SMOCK MILL. A poem by Jeffrey Turner, with a line-block reproduction of a drawing by Mary Norman.
2pp   155 copies   1975   35 signed copies Price 30p, 120 copies Price 15p

SUFFOLK POEMS by Neil Powell, with line-block reproductions of three drawings by Roger Walton.
13pp   140 copies   1975   32 signed copies Price 50p, 95 copies Price 25p   PPB 75.140

TWO BOYS AND A GIRL, PLAYING IN A CHURCHYARD. A poem by Martin Booth, with a linocut by Margaret Steward.
2pp   125 copies   1975   25 signed copies Price 25p, 100 copies Price 15p

WHATEVER THERE IS OF LIGHT. Poems by William Bedford.
3pp   195 copies   1975   35 signed copies   Price 40p, 160 copies Price 20p

DRAGONCARDS, SERIES THREE. Twelve poems by Stewart Conn and eleven other poets.
Twelve cards loosely inserted in envelope, 140 sets   1976   21 signed sets Price £1.50, 119 sets Price 40p

DRAGONCARDS FOUR. Twelve poems by Fleur Adcock and eleven other poets.
Twelve cards loosely inserted in an envelope, about 145 sets   1976   21 signed sets Price £1.50, remainder Price 40p

THE FAILED MINE. Poems by John Gurney, with line-block reproductions of seven drawings by Sally Gurney.
10pp   200 copies   1976   40 signed copies Price 60p, 160 copies Price 40p

A MANDEVILLE FIFTEEN. Poems by Peter Scupham and fourteen other poets.
21pp   250 copies   1976   Price 50p

RIVER PEOPLE. Poems by Joan Downar.
11pp   195 copies   1976   30 signed copies   Price 50p, 165 copies Price 30p

THE ROCK. A poem by John Miller, with a line-block reproduction of a drawing by William Lane.
5pp 200 copies 1976 Price 20p

VISITORS. Poems by George Szirtes, with five etchings by the author. 55 portfolios containing five folders of signed etchings.
1976 45 portfolios for sale Price £5

WATER LANE. Poems by Katherine Middleton, with line-block reproduction of a drawing by Mary Norman.
19pp 250 copies 1976 35 signed copies Price 60p 215 copies Price 40p

A MANDEVILLE TROIKA. Poems by George Szirtes, Neil Powell and Peter Scupham, with a line-block reproduction of a drawing by George Szirtes.
11pp 150 copies 1977 50 signed copies Price 60p, 100 copies Price 30p

A SPRING COLLECTION. Poems by Katherine Middleton and sixteen other poets.
24pp 260 copies 1977 240 copies for sale Price 60p

THE TALES OF ROVER by John Mole, with reproductions of two engravings by Bewick.
12pp 235 copies 1977 35 signed copies Price 90p, 200 copies Price 65p

THE TOPSAIL SCHOONERS by John Gurney, with eleven drawings by Sally Gurney.
16pp 230 copies 1977 30 signed copies Price 65p, 200 copies Price 40p

THE DROWNED RIVER. Poems by Lawrence Sail with two vignettes by Mary Norman.
16pp 250 copies 1978 Price 50p

AN ILLUSTRATED ALPHABET. Poems and etchings by George Szirtes.
30pp 1978 55 signed copies Price £10 Basilisk Catalogue 1 p26

MANDEVILLE DRAGONCARDS FIVE. Poems by Michael Schmidt and eleven other poets.
Twelve cards loosely inserted in envelope   1978   Price 40p
THE OTHER PARISH. Poems by Jeffrey Turner.
16pp   250 copies   1978   Price 50p
YEARS. Sixteen poems by Bernard Bergonzi, with a lineblock reproduction of a drawing by George Szirtes.
24pp   350 copies   1979   Price 50p

THE PLOUGH PRESS
ANAGLYPTOGRAPHY by William John Stannard, with an original anaglyptograph.
ii, 11pp   200 numbered copies printed by Thomas Rae at the Grian-aig Press   1967   Price 12s 6d   PPB 67.129
SHARE OF PLOUGHS. An entertainment of quotations, with eight old electros of wood engravings of ploughs, six used twice, the others three times.
22pp   35 numbered copies   1968   Not for sale   PPB 68.140
LAW & ORDURE, A SQUIB BY 'A NO-GOOD UPPITY NIGGER'
12pp   40 numbered copies   1969   For exchange, not for sale   PPB 69.155
XIX CENTURY ILLUSTRATION. Some methods used in English books, by Geoffrey Wakeman, with about twenty-three specimens of different processes.
77pp prelims + 15 sewn fascicules (31 printed pages in all)   75 numbered copies   1970   72 copies for sale Price £10 10s   PPB 70.147
LOUGHBOROUGH MARBLE. Five specimens of marbled paper.
A single leaf folded zigzag to make 9pp   18 numbered copies   1971   Not for sale   PPB 71.173

THE PAPER MAKER. Reprinted from 'The Book of Trades' [1835]. With a line-block reproduction of a nineteenth century wood engraving.
15pp + tipped-in frontispiece   60 number copies   1971   PPB 71.174

ENGLISH HAND MADE PAPERS SUITABLE FOR BOOKWORK. Assembled by Geoffrey Wakeman, with line-block reproductions of thirteen old engravings, and with a frontispiece leaf made by Wookey Hole Mill watermarked with a picture of a vatman.
76 leaves of which 40 are printed.   75 numbered copies printed on 41 different hand-made papers   1972   Price £20   PPB 72.131

IMPRESSIONS OF BINDER'S TOOLS.
12 leaves printed on rectos only   12 copies   1973   Not for sale   PPB 73.122

ON PRINTING by Loys Le Roi.
11pp   120 copies   1974

PLATES TO ACCOMPANY 'VICTORIAN BOOK ILLUSTRATION' by Geoffrey Wakeman, with twenty specimens of different processes.
44 leaves   23 numbered copies   1974   20 copies for sale   Price £50   PPB 74.99

THE COPPER PLATE PRINTER. With a line-block reproduction of a wood-engraving from the original edition.
10pp   120 copies   1975   100 copies for sale   Price £1   PPB 75.169

THE HISTORY OF F J HEAD & CO by Frederick A Brett.
8pp   120 copies   1975   100 copies for sale   Price £1.25   PPB 75.170

THE PRODUCTION OF 19TH CENTURY COLOUR ILLUSTRATION. Short essays on plates taken from books of the period, by Geoffrey Wakeman.
39pp   100 copies   1976   Price 35

INDIAN HANDMADE PAPERS.
9 folded sheets of paper samples 8 blank and 1 printed, presented loose in paper covers   1977   Price £5   Basilisk Catalogue 1 p33
THE ART OF MAKING PAPER by J de la Lande, introduced by Geoffrey Wakeman and Colin Cohen, with five folding two full page engravings.
31pp   200 copies printed at Skelton's Press Wellingborough 1978   Price £15   Basilisk Catalogue 1 p33
ENGLISH MARBLED PAPERS, A documentary history, by Geoffrey Wakeman.
32pp and 26 sample leaves   112 copies printed at Skelton's Press, Wellingborough   1978   Price £50
PAAS & COOK: PROVINCIAL BOOKBINDING IN THE 1830s by Frances Docker.
1979   Price £15

POET & PRINTER
POETRY FROM THE PEOPLE. Edited by Ken Geering.
25pp   750 copies printed for publication by Breakthru Publications, Sussex   1965   PPB 67.130
THE SWAN AND OTHER POEMS by Gordon J Blundell.
16pp   about 80 copies   1965   Price 2s   PPB 67.132
WORDS FROM THE LAND OF THE LIVING by Colin R Fry.
20pp   about 100 copies   1965   Price 2s   PPB 67.131
THE QUARREL WITH OURSELVES. Verse by Barry Tebb.
20pp   about 114 copies   1966   Price 2s   PPB 67.133
The three pamphlets above were printed free of charge and given to the poets concerned to do with as they wished. The Poet & Printer imprint first appeared in Peter Redgrove's 'Sermon' listed below.
THE SERMON by Peter Redgrove.
15pp   500 copies   1966   Price 2s   PPB 66.127

FIVE QUIET SHOUTERS. An anthology of assertive verse, edited by Barry Tebb.
35pp   350 copies   1966   Price 2s   PPB 66.129
THE WORDS OF CHRISTOPHER LOGUE'S ESTABLISHMENT SONGS, ETCETERA.
19pp   350 copies   1966   Price 2s 6d   PPB 66.128
FIFTY EPIPHYTES by Jonathan Williams.
16pp   600 copies   1967   Price 3s   PPB 67.135
ONE LITTLE PRESS YEAR. Portfolio collating the first four Poet & Printer pamphlets.
55 copies   1967   Price 10s 6d
POEMS by Francis Horovitz.
16pp   526 copies printed for publication by St Alberts Press, Aylesford   1967   26 signed copies Price £1 1s, 500 copies Price 2s 6d   PPB 67.136
SCAPEGOATS AND RABIES by Ted Hughes.
14pp   400 copies   1967   Price 2s   PPB 67.134
FAMILY TREE. A collection of modern verse by A E Dudley
16pp   about 350 copies   1968   Price 2s   PPB 68.143
NOSTALGIA NEUROSIS & OTHER POEMS by Penelope Shuttle, with a half-tone reproduction of a photograph of the author printed on the back cover.
16pp   526 copies   1968   26 signed copies   Price £1 1s, 500 copies Price 3s 2d   PPB 68.142
THE OLD WHITE MAN. A poem adapted from a Chinese Tang Dynasty story by Peter Redgrove with a line-block reproduction of a drawing by Rigby Graham.
10pp   24 copies   1968   Not for sale   PPB 68.144
THREE REGIONAL VOICES by Iain Crichton Smith, Barry Tebb, and Michael Longley.
36pp   450 copies   1968   Price 3s   PPB 68.141
GALLERY. Poems by John Stevens Wade, with line-block reproductions of 14 drawings by Tom Ricciardi.
31pp   500 copies   1969   Price 6s   PPB 69.157

PRIVATE TIME, PUBLIC TIME. Fifteen poems by Robert Shaw, with a line-block reproduction of a drawing by Rigby Graham.
31pp   400 copies   1969   Price 3s   PPB 69.158
RAIN. A prose-poem translated from the French of Francis Ponge by Peter Hoy.
A single sheet   90 copies   1969   Not for sale
WORK IN PROGRESS. Poems by Peter Redgrove.
60pp   400 copies   1969   26 signed copies, Price £2 10s, 370 copies, Price 13s 6d   PPB 69.156
CROSS-CURRENTS. Poems by Barry Tebb.
28pp   about 400 copies   1970   Price 6s   PPB 70.148
DEATH OF CAEDMON. A poem by Ian Caws.
A single sheet   100 copies given to the poet   100 copies printed on a variety of off-cuts for free distribution by the printer   1970
PORTFOLIO. SECOND LITTLE PRESS YEAR. Running from Spring 1969 to Spring 1970 and edited by Poet & Printer with line-block reproductions of three drawings by Tom Ricciardi and one, in two sizes, by Rigby Graham.
22pp   40 copies   1970   Price £1 10s   PPB 70.150
READING POEMS OVER BRANDY. A poem for Alan Dixon by W Price Turner.
A single sheet   100 copies   1970   Unpriced
TRANSMISSIONS. Poems by Malcolm Ritchie with illustrations by the poet.
22pp   350 copies   1970   Price 3s
THE UPRIGHT POSITION. Poems by Alan Dixon.
44pp   450 copies printed by the Magpie Press, London 1970   Price 8s   PPB 70.151
CROW WAKES. Poems by Ted Hughes.
27pp   230 copies   1971   30 copies not for sale, but presented for academic or review purposes, 100 copies presented to the poet, 100 copies for sale, Price £2.25   PPB 71.175

APPLE PEOPLE by Alan Tucker, with two double-page and two single-page lithographs by Rigby Graham.
30pp   450 copies   1972   Price £1   PPB 72.134
LARES. Poems by Michael Longley, with line-block reproductions of three drawings by Brian Ferran.
23pp   400 copies   1972   Price 20p   PPB 72.132
THREE PIECES FOR VOICES by Peter Redgrove.
23pp   500 copies   1972   Price 24p   PPB 72.133
TELLER. Four poems by Martin Booth.
15pp   400 copies   1973   Price 20p   PPB 73.123
FISHING IN THE SKY. Love poems by Michael Longley, with reproductions of two photographic and montage illustrations by John Middleton, and a photograph of the poet by Laurencine Lot.
24pp   500 copies   1975   Price 50p   PPB 75.172
ROBERT SHAW'S WORK IN PROGRESS with two woodcuts by Alan Dixon.
84pp   410 copies   1975   Price £1.50   PPB 75.171
BEGINNINGS. Poems by Eric Walter White.
30pp   in hardback and paperback formats   Price, hardback £1.80   1976
THE FIRST ELEVEN. A collection of poems by Gavin Ewart.
20pp   1977   Price 60p
THE EGOTISTICAL DECLINE. Poems by Alan Dixon, with a woodcut by the author.
24pp   1978   Price 60p
BRUISED MADONNA. A collection of poems by Ian Caws, with a line-block of Madonna and child on the cover and title page, which has been copied from the Wilton Diptych.
30pp   1979   Price 60p

THE SHOESTRING PRESS
JONAH, A TALE FROM THE BIBLE illustrated with linocuts and bound with hand-made marbled papers produced by Ben Sands. 1956
THE WALRUS AND THE CARPENTER. Illustrated with coloured linocuts by Ben Sands. 1958
MY PATH by Charles Evans, illustrated by Ben Sands.
11pp   150 copies   1959   Price 4s 6d   PPB 59.69
THE DRAGON OF WANTLEY. A rendition in Regency dress of a burlesque opera in three acts by Henry Carey, illustrated by Ben Sands.
32pp   200 signed copies   1960   Price by subscription £1 1s, Price through booksellers £1 10s   PPB 60.88
THE TRAGICAL DEATH OF A APPLE PIE. A traditional alphabet edited and illustrated with linocuts by Ben Sands.
28 leaves printed on one side only, joined and folded to make a twelve-foot long concertina and retained in loose brown paper wrappers   225 signed copies   1966   Price   1 2s 6d   PPB 66.136
DICK AND SAL AT CANTERBURY FAIR. Early 19th century poem in the Kentish dialect by John White Masters with a bibliographical note by Christopher Buckingham, with two linocuts by Ben Sands.
12pp   228 numbered copies signed by the artist   1973   Price £2.20   PPB 73.145
A DISSERTATION UPON ROAST PIG by Charles Lamb, with five linocuts and linocut lettering by Ben Sands.
12pp   70 numbered copies signed by the artist   1975   about 50 copies for sale   Price £4.20   PPB 75.204

Index

Adana (Printing Machines) Ltd 18
'Albion', journal 87
Albion Press 17
Allenholme Press 57-59
Aloes Books 90
Amateur Printers Association 51
'The American Book Collector' 54
'Antiquarian Book Monthly Review' 87
Ark Press 57
Arts and Crafts Movement 19, 21-23, 27
Arts Council of Gt. Britain 130-131
Ashdene Press 27-28
Association of Little Presses 72

Basilisk Press and Bookshop 12, 95, 96, 124-126, 131
'Basilisk Press & Bookshop Catalogue 1' 126, 130
Batchelor, Joseph, papermaker 23, 24, 48
'The Black Art', journal 53-54
Black Knight Press 64-65
Blake, William 10, 16-17
Bland, David 29-30
'Book Design and Production' 51, 53
'The Book of the Private Press' 50, 67
Bookselling, private press books 125-126, 131-133
Booth, Martin 73
Brace, William R 51
Brewhouse broadsheets 63
Brewhouse Press 62-63, 83-86
British Printing Society 51
Brownjohn, Alan 78
Brunskill, Ann 90
Burford Mason, Roger 87, 119

Campbell, Duine 64-65
Carter, John 54
Carter, Sebastian 45
Carter, Will 43-45
'Catalogue of Little Presses in Print' 72-73

Caton, Reginald 67
Cave, Roderick 9-10, 17-18, 42, 49, 53, 73, 81
Cellar Press Poets 120
Chambers, David 52, 55, 95, 97-99
Chambers, Harry 119
Chiswick Press 21, 29
Chubb, Ralph 35-37
Cleverdon, Douglas 45
Clodd, Alan 73
Clover Hill Editions 45
Cobden-Sanderson, T J 24-27
Cog Press 63-64
Cope, R W 17
Cowan, Louis 45
Cowper, Edward 18
Cox, Morris 65-66, 129
Crescendo Poetry Series 42, 68
Cuckoo Hill Press 55, 95, 97-99

Daedalus Press 73
Daniel, C H O 10, 19-21
Distribution, private press books 129-133
Dodman Press 87
Doves Press 24-27

Ede, Charles 46
Enitharmon Press 73
Exhibitions:
  Brewhouse Press, Clarkesville, Tennessee 1973 83-86
  'English Private Presses 1757-1961', London 1961 54
  17th King's Lynn Festival, 1967 79-80
  'The Page Right Printed', Glasgow 1973 83
  'The Private Press', Loughborough 1968 80-81
  Swiss Cottage Library, 1976 86
  Watford, 1969 81-82
  Watford, 1970 82-83

Fairbank, Alfred 108
Fairfax Hall, B 32-33
Fantasy Poets 69-70

166

Index

Fantasy Press 68-70
Fell types 20
Fiction publishing 90-91, 107
Folio Society 46
Fortune Press 67
Foster, Peter 47-48
Franklin, Colin 34
'The Franklin Press' 59

Gaberbocchus Press 72
Gage-Cole, H 32
Garry, Charlene 95, 124-126
Gibbings, Robert 29
Gill, Eric 29, 30, 33, 82
'Glossary of the Book' 9
Gogmagog Press 65-66, 129
Golden Cockerel Press 28-29, 31
Golden Head Press 47
Graham, Rigby 61-64, 74
Green, Patricia 62
Grian-aig Press 56
Guthrie, James 33-35

Hamilton Finlay, Ian 71
Hand and Flower Press 68
Handley-Taylor, Geoffrey 50
Hardacre, Kenneth 51, 52, 55, 82, 95, 108-112
Hartley, George 68
Hickman, Trevor 62-63, 83-86
Hobbs, Jack 70
Hodgkiss, Peter 72
Holtzapffel & Co 18
Horsfall, Julia 88, 91, 131
Hughes, Olwen 89-90

International Small Printers Association 51
Isaac, Peter C G 57-59

Jackson, Holbrook 26
Jenson, Nicholas 23, 27
Johnston, Edward 27

Keepsake Poems 107
Keepsake Press 55, 78, 91, 95, 105-107
Kelmscott Press 19, 22-24

Kirgate, Thomas 15
Kit-Cat Press 55, 95, 108-112

Latin Press 38-43, 68
Lewis, Roy 55, 78, 90, 95, 105-107
Lichfield, Boyd 74
Linocutting 100-101
Lister, Raymond 47
London Chappel 52
Lucie-Smith, Edward 72
Lunatic Fringe Publications 90

McBride, Ralph 131
Mandeville Press 78, 95, 119-121, 130
Marketing, private press books 129-133
Martin, Douglas 61-62
Marvell Press 67-68
Marx, Erica 68
Mason, John 60-61
Melissa Press 38
Mellor, Oscar 68-70
Merrion Press 59
Midgely Taylor, Harold 28-29
'Miniature Folio of Private Presses' 50-51
Miniature Press 49-50
Model Four hand-platen press 100
Model Printing Press Co 18
Mole, John 119-121
Moran, James 53
Morris, Guido 38-43, 68
Morris, William 10, 19, 22-24

New Broom Private Press 74-75

Orpheus Press 61-62

Pandora Press 62
Parlour press 18, 19
Parlour printing 17-18
Parry, Nicholas & Mary 90
Pear Tree Press 33-35
Perpetua Press 29-30
Peters, John 47-48

Phoenix broadsheets 75
Phoenix poetry pamphlets 119
Piech, Paul Peter 52, 81, 88-89
Plough Press 95, 116-117, 130
Poet & Printer 78, 95, 113-115, 130
'Poetry Information', journal 72
Poetry publishing 67-78, 105-107, 113-115, 119-121
Potocki, Geoffrey, Count Potocki of Montalk 37-39
Prince, Edward P, punch cutter 23, 27
'The Printing Art', journal 87
'Printing for Pleasure' 49-50
Private Libraries Association 51-53
'The Private Library', journal 52
'The Private Press' 9
'The Private Press: Handbook to an Exhibition' 81
'Private Press Books', bibliography 53, 130
'The Private Press in Hertfordshire' 82
'Private Presses & Their Books' 11
'Private Printer & Private Press', journal 87

Rae, Thomas 50, 53, 55-56
Rainbow Press 89-90
Rampant Lions Press 43-45
Randle, John & Rosalind 89
Ransom, Will 11, 54-55
Ridler, Vivian 29-30
Robinson, William 15
Rolph, John 70
Ryder, John 9, 49-51

St Bride Printing Library 12
St John Hornby, C H 27-29, 33
Sandford, Christopher 29, 31, 32
Sands, Ben 55, 96, 100-104
Savage, Toni 62, 74-75
Sceptre Press 73
Scorpion Press 70-71
Scupham, Peter 78, 95, 119-121, 130
Shaw, Susan 59
Shoestring Press 55, 96, 100-104
Signet Press 55-56
'Small Printer', journal 86
Society of Private Printers 51-52
Society of Wood Engravers 29
Standing, Juliet 73, 80
Stanhope, 3rd Earl of 17
Stourton Press 32-33
Strawberry Hill Press 15

Tarling, Alan 78, 95, 113-115, 130
Taurus Press of Willow Dene 88-89
Taylor, Kim 57
Tern Press 90
Themerson, Stefan 72-73
Transican Books 74

Vine Press 47-48

Wakeman, Geoffrey 95, 116-117, 130
Walker, Emery 22-28
Walpole, Horace 15-16
Whittington Press 89
Wild Hawthorn Press 71
Worden, Kenneth, printer 42, 57
World's End Press 90

Zapf, Herman 44, 108